MEMOS
FROM
MIDLIFE

MEMOS FROM MIDLIFE

24 Parables of Adult Adjustment

Franklin E. Zimring

QUID PRO BOOKS
New Orleans, Louisiana

Copyright © 2015 by Franklin E. Zimring. All rights reserved. No part of this book may be reproduced by any mechanical, photographic, or electronic process, or other recording, nor may it be stored in a retrieval system, transmitted, or otherwise copied for public or private use—other than for "fair use" or excerpts in reviews—without the written permission of the publisher.

Published in 2015 by Quid Pro Books.

ISBN 978-1-61027-296-4 (pbk.)
ISBN 978-1-61027-299-5 (hbk.)
ISBN 978-1-61027-298-8 (ebk.)

QUID PRO BOOKS
Quid Pro, LLC
5860 Citrus Blvd., suite D-101
New Orleans, Louisiana 70123
www.quidprobooks.com

qp

Publisher's Cataloging-in-Publication

Zimring, Franklin E.
    Memos from midlife : 24 parables of adult adjustment / Franklin E. Zimring.
        p. cm. — (Journeys and memoirs)
    ISBN 978-1-61027-296-4 (pbk.)

1. Aging. 2. Middle age—Humor. 3. Conduct of life. I. Title. II. Series
PN6231.R3Z21 2015   812' .25.7—dc22
                                                                                                2015846398
                                                                                                                    CIP

Front cover artwork, a sketch of the author, copyright © 2014 by Carole Peel, all rights reserved. Used by permission and with the thanks of the author and publisher. Author photograph on 'About the Author' page courtesy of Michal Crawford Zimring. Cover design © 2015 by Quid Pro, LLC. See also 'Credits' page for more permissions.

Second Quid Pro Books printing, October 2015.

CONTENTS

Introduction i

Acknowledgments iii

Care and Feeding 1

Love and Family 21

Success and Failure American Style 41

Origins and Influence 79

The Psychology of Commerce 101

About the Author 125

Introduction

These essays differ from most nonfiction writing in two respects—subject matter and method. In the age of the op-ed and the blog, millions of essays are written on hundreds of thousands of topics. But most of this endless variety of written expression concerns the outside world and how it should be run. Politics, economics, public policy, fashion, social values and world affairs are the usual focus of the worlds' pundits. Most of my own published writing has also been dedicated to sharing my expertise on the hot issues in my professional life. So if any who read this are interested in what Frank Zimring thinks of capital punishment or the war on drugs or trends in crime rates, Mr. Google can quickly guide them to a number of my writings on such topics.

But not in these pages. This book is a report from my second career, and everybody else's second career. It concerns the meanings and lessons that come from the hard work of becoming an adult in the modern world. For a period that began near the dawn of my early middle age and has continued since then, the events and insights of becoming and continuing to act as an adult have produced a series of essays that are the "memos from midlife" announced in the title of this volume.

So this is an autobiography? Absolutely not. Neither the events of my adulthood nor the lessons that emerged from them are in any sense remarkable. Quite the opposite in fact: the major themes of my adult life—choices, children, the necessity and limits of love, self-discipline, ambition and disappointment—are common, almost universal aspects of adulthood. Autobiographies, at least those that keep their readers awake, are organized around individually remarkable events, while the essays in this volume concern the lessons most people have to learn and do learn in order to conduct constructive lives. What do you say when your eight-year-old asks whether you would save him or his sister if there was only room for one of them in a life boat? How should you feel about the people who continue to smoke once you have finally succeeded in quitting, and why? What makes us feel proud of being frequent flying club members? Why is loving someone the opposite of being powerful? Why do professors who hate to teach their students love to go anywhere else to give a speech? Why is nostalgia in one important sense an arrogant emotion? The topics in this collection concern the common wisdom we acquire in living as grown-ups in a complicated world. It is everybody's autobiography.

The peculiar methodology of these essays is the parable. The usual dictionary definition of parable is a short allegorical story designed to illustrate some truth, principle or moral lesson. The pages that follow are chock full of allegorical stories, metaphors and comparative constructs within the common boundaries of the domain of the parable. My heavy reliance on parable is not an after-the-fact strategy to communicate lessons acquired by other means, but reflects instead the way I came to understand the particular principles under consideration. These parables of adult adjustment reflect my way of thinking about these questions and are not merely strategies for reporting my conclusions. Much of my adult life has presented itself to me as a series of story problems, and these essays track the paths I took to insight. The Sistine Chapel was in fact part of my introduction to the dilemma of landmarks, and looking for a parking space was an element in my learning how variable our priorities can become.

The parable has both strengths and weaknesses as a method of learning. The power of an insight should be evident in the story that conveys it. But if lessons are presented in this fashion, adulthood as thus understood is hardly an exact science. The lessons learned from parables are soft at the edges; the solutions to puzzles are often distressingly partial. Many of the problems don't have solutions. And the many different parables on many different issues do not add up to any comprehensive model or map of adult life.

Comprehensive accounts of the rules of adult life require an ideology or orthodox religious belief that has not yet captured my conviction. These essays are for the eclectic and agnostic who cannot see the entirety of adult life as a detailed and deductive code of conduct, and instead learn their life lessons one at a time. This is not a quick or economical way to grow up, but it does seem authentic.

Franklin E. Zimring

Acknowledgments

The accumulation of these essays over a sustained period of time was supported by long-term and short-term benefactors. The early encouragement came from a trio of mentors who both inspired and encouraged the enterprise: Maury Zimring, John Walsh, and Gordon Hawkins. Jan Vetter and Meir Dan-Cohen tolerated early versions of many of the essays in this collection (and several that didn't survive their generous critiques). Alan Childress and Dani McClellan each contributed cheerfully to creating a volume that aspires to be greater than the sum of its parts. Karen Chin produced many of the essays in draft form in the 1980s and 1990s. Toni Mendicino assisted in keeping the project organized and on schedule.

Credits

The illustrations in Chapters 2, 4, 5, and 20 were produced by Phil McAndrew and are copyright © 2014 by Phil McAndrew.

The illustration in Chapter 10 is reprinted by permission of *CHEMTECH*, June 1988, 16(6) OBC. Copyright © 1999 American Chemical Society.

The illustration in Chapter 11 (and back cover inset) is reprinted by permission of Debbie Drechsler.

The advertisement that illustrates Chapter 13 is reproduced with the permission of Brandwagon, the Marketing Club of the Indian Institute of Foreign Trade.

Earlier versions of five chapters were first published as follows:

> Chapter 2 in "My Turn," *Newsweek*, April 20, 1987
>
> Chapter 9 in *Moment*, Vol. 6 (1980), p. 58
>
> Chapter 10 in *The New York Times*, April 20, 1987, p. 19, and the *International Herald Tribune*, April 23, 1987, p. 5
>
> Chapter 11 in *California Monthly*, April 1991
>
> Chapter 24 in the *San Francisco Chronicle*, April 21, 2013, p. E6.

MEMOS
FROM
MIDLIFE

CARE AND FEEDING

1 · The Prince of Wales Should Probably Shave Himself

2 · The Psychological World of the Former Smoker

3 · The Piranha Theory of Overcommitment

4 · Human Existence as an Eating Disorder

1
The Prince of Wales Should Probably Shave Himself

I can date my disillusionment with the allure of shows like the "Lifestyles of the Rich and Famous" to an afternoon, in East Lansing, Michigan, when I treated myself to a barbershop straight razor shave for the first (and only) time. I had been looking forward to this expensive adventure. What could be more luxurious than taking an onerous daily task, a thankless self-responsibility, and for just one day putting it in the hands of a skilled professional?

There was a 1940s movie romance to the ritual of preparation that got matters off to an encouraging start, with five minute devoted to a succession of hot towels for the softening of the customer's whiskers. By and large, however, my professional shave was a disappointment to me. The barbershop version took anywhere from three to five times longer than shaving myself. While that time investment might be justified as a one-time ritual, it holds zero promise as a daily routine. Being shaved is also not a particularly comfortable experience because of the attention one has to devote to making oneself available for the ministration of others.

There was one other problem with my East Lansing experiment with luxury: it wasn't a particularly great shave. It was smooth in sections on the flat, but there were residual patches of stubble in hard-to-reach corners. The barber's skill was clearly superior to mine. But the level of difficulty of his task, the sheer difficulty of shaving someone else when compared to exploring one's own familiar nooks and crannies, meant that, when it comes one's own face, an untalented amateur can match the quality of a professional's work.

It turns out that a barbershop shave is simultaneously expensive, time consuming, hard work for the customer, and not quite as good as the do-it-yourself variety. Under these circumstances, I share a fate dictated by circumstances with the Prince of Wales and he with me: we both should probably shave ourselves. He has to shave himself because the alternative is too damn much trouble. Whatever else might comprise the lifestyles of the rich and famous, the daily shave seems by its nature one of life's nondelegable duties. And it is only one on a very long list.

There are so many things we can only do for ourselves that coming to terms with life's long list of nondelegable duties is a central task of every adult. We cannot commission a surrogate to get a good night's sleep for us, to quit smoking, to floss our teeth, to relax, or to lose ten pounds. These are not small matters. In relatively rare circumstances, others can teach us things. But other people cannot learn things for us, and learning life's lessons is something very much different and more important than having them taught. The qualities of mind and body, of mood, attention, and perspective that determine the quality of each person's day, are things we must bring to our lives single-handedly. Comics can tell us jokes, but nobody else can cheer us up or calm us down.

One other personal task of central importance cannot be delegated: choosing the path of one's life in a free society. Making choices in life is often harder than shaving with cold water, but we can only avoid the responsibility for our own decisions by denying that who we are as individuals is important to the way we should live our lives.

A visceral realization of the nondelegability of life's important duties teaches other lessons as well. It emphasizes how much of our existence is living out a common human condition. Imagining a daily battle in front of the shaving mirror as the shared fate of Prince Charles and myself should diminish my envy of those many things that differentiate my life from his. The most important adversaries for each of us, biological and psychological, are enemies of us all. The good news about our common fate, the biologic rout that all too soon awaits us, is that it should generate fellow feeling.

The long list of life's nondelegable duties also teaches that self-discipline is a survival virtue necessary in everyone's life. There is literally no substitute for the self-regard that prompts us to postpone pleasure and invest effort. And there is no skill more important than the capacity to exercise self-discipline. If your children learn nothing else, let them learn this: they cannot be too rich to need discipline, or too smart, or too charming.

Just as the wide variety of nondelegable life duties should be a democratic force in society, it is also an important counterweight to our tendency to imagine ourselves as terribly specialized in modern life. The wide variety of things we must do for ourselves pushes each of us to participate in a broader spectrum of activities with many more common elements than might otherwise happen. Because no investment analysts are either smart enough or rich enough to hire someone else to take their exercise for them, they must become exercisers themselves and not just investment analysts. Having a whole variety of tasks to do ourselves makes us more various as well as more like one another. And this is good news, even if we have to shave ourselves.

At the core of life's nondeligable duties is the need to take care of oneself. It is no accident that the pioneer institution to support facilities and training for the physically handicapped in Berkeley calls itself the Center for Independent Living. Those who have had limits placed on their capacity to do things for themselves are the first to recognize that independence is central, a sine qua non.

So everybody needs his or her own Center for Independent Living. We depend on the help of others to learn effectively to help ourselves, but we must become freestanding, to an extraordinary extent, before we can conduct the right kind of adult life.

One final point to make about my discovery that it is necessary in this life to shave oneself. The insight is a simple one. I had my barbershop adventure at age twenty-one, but the rather simple generalization of the experience took perhaps two decades longer to surface in my life. What took me so long?

Growing up tends to take a long time for most people. And the slow learning process of growing up is impossible to outsource. You cannot hire anyone either to grow up for you or to teach you maturation in ten easy steps. Often our real choice is between learning simple things slowly or never at all. And my career as a slow learner provides the inspiration for the pages that follow.

2
The Psychological World of the Former Smoker

The world is not divided into two groups, smokers and nonsmokers, but rather into three: those who smoke, those who have never smoked, and the curious and growing group of us who live our lives as ex-smokers. The former smoker and the nonsmoker may stay on the same floors of hotels, but they live in different worlds. The nonsmoker literally does not know what he or she is missing. The former smoker will never forget. For those who have never smoked, the fact of being a nonsmoker may be either important or not as an element of personal identity. But being a former smoker is for almost all of us an important part of who we are.

Ex-smokers are veterans of a personal war that cannot be fully understood by either smokers or nonsmokers. The former smoker has been transformed, and linked to other former smokers, by the watershed experience of ceasing to smoke, and by the temptation to recidivate. The ex-smoker is much closer in psychology to the active smoker, but the former smoker may feel a need to scorn smokers in the world around him and to deny the smoker in himself. Two key dimensions—the relation of former smokers to other smokers and to themselves—shape the different psychological modes of ex-smokers. Smokers who have quit adapt one of four different psychological styles: the zealot, the evangelist, the elect, and the serene.

Not all anti-tobacco zealots we encounter are former smokers, but a substantial number of the fire-and-brimstone opponents of smoking and smokers have been recruited from the ranks of the reformed. The zealot believes that those who continue to smoke are a degenerate enemy camp, more to be scorned than pitied. Punishment rather than therapy are the zealot's prescription of choice for those who continue to smoke. Relations between these people and those close to them who continue to smoke are strained.

A major explanation of zealots' intensity is their tenuous hold on their own abstinence. Part of the emotional force derives from sheer envy as they watch and identify with every lung-filling puff. Thus, the forceful condemnation of other smokers is an effort to enforce the taboo against themselves. To admit the humanity of those who continue to smoke they must confront the possibility that they are also at risk of recidivism. By making smoking a crime of the sub-human, zealots seek reassurance that it cannot happen to them.

No systematic survey has been done on the subject, but my impression is that those ex-smokers who have become zealots include a disproportionate number of the thousands of doctors who have quit. And many of today's most vitriolic zealots also include those who have been the most deeply committed to tobacco habits. Just as the most enthusiastic revolutionary tends to make the most enthusiastic anti-revolutionary, there seems to be a reaction formation to be observed in the war on tobacco.

The anti-smoking evangelists spend an enormous amount of time seeking out and preaching to the unconverted, but differ from the zealot because they do not condemn smokers. The evangelist regards smoking as a social disease rather than a sin, an easily curable morbid condition that stands between his or her audience and heaven on earth. Evangelists argue that quitting the habit is only mildly difficult. After all, they did it. Moreover, they describe the benefits of quitting as beyond measure and the disadvantages as nonexistent. So quitting is easy and obvious—all that current smokers need to do is give it a try.

The hallmark of evangelistic ex-smokers is their insistence that they never miss tobacco. Although they are less hostile to smoking associates than the zealot, they are frequently even more resented. Friends and loved ones who have been the targets of preachment frequently greet the return to smoking of an evangelist as an occasion for unmitigated glee.

The distinction between anti-smoking evangelists and the self-defined elect among former smokers parallels the distinction between proselytizing and nonproselytizing religious sects. While evangelistic former smokers preach the ease and desirability of abstinence, elected former smokers do not regard their current virtue as a contagious condition and do not attempt to spread it among their friends. Instead, the elect among ex-smokers subscribe to a belief that parallels the puritan theory of predetermination. They have proved capable of abstaining from tobacco, but they are probably different from those of their friends and relations who continue to smoke. These nonsmokers rarely give personal testimony about their conversion. The elect among former smokers do not frequently speak of their smoking histories while former smoker evangelists rarely talk of anything else. Of course, active smokers find this kind of tobacco-oriented Calvinism far less obnoxious than either the evangelist or the zealot. Yet the self-appointed elect ex-smokers are often resented for their smugness, for the palpable air of self-satisfaction that rarely escapes notice when others light up. For active smokers, living with a member of the ex-smoking elect is less openly conflictual than with zealots or evangelists, but subtly oppressive nonetheless.

My final type of former smokers, the serene, should encourage those who are moved close to despair by the obvious obnoxiousness of the other psychic styles of ex-smokers. True serenity is quieter than zealotry and evangelism, and less self-righteous than those who define themselves as elect in their own tobacco abstinence. The serene ex-smoker accepts those around him who continue to smoke without imposing the psychological distance of scorn or feeling the need to disidentify.

This kind of serenity does not seem to be an initial option for those who quit smoking, but rather is an end stage in a process of development when some former smokers progress through one or more of the less positive psychological adaptations and then grow up. Serenity is the good news that happens when the zealot calms down and the evangelist develops other interests. Serenity is thus a positive possibility that exists at the end of the Ericksonian rainbow for former smokers, but by no means do all former smokers reach that psychic promised land.

What is there that permits some former smokers to reach serenity? I think the key here is self-acceptance and gratitude. Fully mature former smokers know that they have the soul of an addict and are grateful for that knowledge. Even though they never need to huddle in the increasingly constricted smoker's ghettos of modern life, their hearts are still in the smoking section. They do not regret either that they quit smoking or their previous adventures with tobacco. To be truly serene about one's status as a former smoker is to be grateful for the experience, cravings, and memories. Serenity lies in this gratitude for the lessons of living one's life as one has lived it, for the acceptance of one's particular history. This former smoker believes that it is better to crave (one hopes only occasionally) and not to smoke than never to have craved at all. With that, the ex-smoker need not excoriate, envy, or disassociate.

And those who have reached serenity in their world view as ex-smokers have much to be grateful for. They have learned both the potential and limits of human change. The experience of becoming the right kind of former smoker thus makes us more fully realized as human beings.

3
The Piranha Theory of Overcommitment

In that great swimming pool of life, those potential predators who model their behavior on the pattern of that innocent looking little South American fish, the piranha, are far more dangerous to the control of your destiny than those who act like the great white shark.

Approaching a swimming pool that contains a man-eating shark, we are forewarned if not forearmed when we are invited in for a swim. This fish looks like he wants to consume us, and none but the suicidal will voluntarily swim with him. Once we have tiptoed past the age of vulnerability to religious cults and army recruiters, most of us have learned to be polite but firm with the obvious sharks in our path. Those who ask for 100 percent of our time and effort send rather obvious warning signs.

But the piranha is a small fish that can sound like he's making a modest request. As we peer into his pool, the invitation sounds less threatening. "Come swim with me, I'll only take a few bites." After all, this little fish only needs a relatively small proportion of your corpus for sustenance. It's much harder to turn the little fellow down.

The problem, of course, is that there are 2,000 piranha in the pool. And by the time a pack of them are finished with you, each only taking small bites, your bones have been picked clean far beyond the most ravenous shark's ambition. This is the Piranha Theory of Over-Commitment, and it is the path most of us take to lives that are beyond our control. The mathematics of the piranha are obvious, but the psychology of defending against these critters is quite difficult to master.

The cumulative dangers of the human version of the pool full of piranha are well known. For many of us, however, forewarned is not forearmed. We are constantly losing control over our priorities and our schedules to people who wish only an hour or an evening, who need just ten pages, or a short trip. A series of small extortions can break the bank just as certainly as one major heist, but there is something that retards our ability to thoroughly learn this lesson. Why do most of us remain so easily the prey of human piranha?

One useful window into why we are so vulnerable to piecemeal overcommitment comes from exploring the modus operandi of those who consistently exploit. There are three key elements to the creed of human piranha. They ask only small favors, they don't want to hurt you, and they believe that any larger harm you suffer from the cumulative impact of them and all their peers is your fault rather than theirs. Each element in this worldview is of importance to the piranha's gambit.

The human piranha only asks small favors, for the kinds of sacrifice that all of us can make from time to time: the one-day trip, the Tuesday evening, or just an hour or two. And the affordability of the sacrifice that each asks is the distinguishing characteristic of the piranha's ploy. There is also an appeal to vanity here: one reason we can afford to give is that we have so much. "Daddy, you're rich," begins the importuning child, acting as an aspiring piranha.

The modesty of the request is also an important part of the human piranha's definition of the relationship between him and his mark. Sharks, by the nature of their request, are your natural enemies. It is difficult indeed for those who want to eat me to view themselves as my friends. But because each piranha, working individually, only wants a few bites, they can each see themselves as friends and fans. Indeed, they would not want a few little bites from me especially if they were not my greatest admirers. Each nibble is a token of their high regard. I should take this attention as a compliment.

But how can the piranha persist in saying that he or she does not want to hurt me when we are both aware that there are many piranha in the pool, and that when I give in to enough of them, my bones will have been picked clean.

The key here, the way in which the human piranha avoids moral responsibility for the cumulative impact of all the piranha in the pool is this: each fish is unique in his or her own eyes. Every piranha in the receiving line we encounter sees themselves as distinguishable from all of the others, and therefore singular in the moral virtue of his request. So the cumulative impact of saying yes too many times is not their problem. It is mine.

It is painfully obvious that a week that includes five meetings in five different cities will be an exhausting waste of time and an impossible period to do any thinking or substantive work. But even as that big admirer of yours who consumed your Tuesday shakes his or her head sadly at the ruin of your schedule, he or she is guilt free and believes that Toledo on Tuesday was this week's one meeting truly worth your effort. And it is therefore your inability to restrict your schedule to such truly deserving destinations that got you in trouble. Any sign of overcommittment is evidence that you have poor judgment about the requests of all those other piranha. As long as he or she is, by his or her definition, the only qualified recipient of your largesse, it is your own fault if you are picked clean by a pool full of undeserving fish. Can't you tell the difference between the truly deserving piranha and the rest of those in the pool?

It is this self-righteousness that is the signature of the successfully predatory piranha. As usual, therefore, when trying to control our efforts and agenda, our most dangerous enemies turn out to be those who can proceed with the moral self-assurance that they are really our friends.

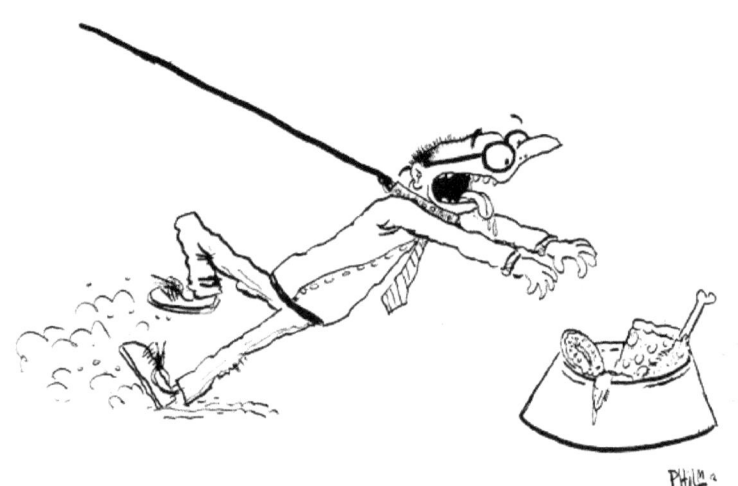

4
Human Existence as an Eating Disorder

One doesn't have to intern at an advertising agency to know that terms like "normal" and "natural" are chock-full of positive and healthy connotations. Mother nature is after all the architect of our life cycle, so "all natural" ingredients are obviously superior to their unnatural competitors. And if natural is the top-of-the-line for life's comestibles, then "normal" is by far the healthiest way to use mother nature's portfolio of good things to eat, drink and wear. The path to well-being and moderation in this adjectival construct is to use our human appetites and instincts in a normal and natural fashion.

And when things do go wrong in wonderland, the obvious reason is usually seen to be a departure from the normal and the natural. Outbreaks of child and adult obesity in recent years have inspired an energetic search for the outside pathological forces that have disturbed the equilibrium of human nutrition. From this perspective, the easy path back to slim boys and girls is to restore normality. In one version of this lament Ronald McDonald has robbed our youth of their normal capacity to self-regulate their food choices, caloric intake and weight. All we need to do is restore our children (and their rapidly thickening parents) to that nutritional Garden of Eden where human nature can work its happy magic.

Bollocks! Relying on human nature to regulate healthy eating and drinking habits is perversely wrongheaded. For most varieties of dysfunctional eating and drinking, far from being the solution, human nature is the heart of the problem.

Let's talk drinking. Even since alcohol was invented, the natural trajectory for its human users has been to get stupidly drunk. In the best statistical sense, then, moderate drinking is an unnatural act.

And moderate eating? In circumstances where there are ample supplies of appetizing food, the natural instincts of human animals drive them to eat far more food and far more fat than is required to maintain a constant body weight. The modern institutional inventions to facilitate such human gluttony are numerous--the all-you-can-eat restaurant comes in both buffet and table service modes and has a provenance that stretches centuries before the advent of fast food. The demand for too much to eat precedes the supply. Whether or not these eating preferences served some ancient evolutionary imperative, they are as fattening as hell.

One powerful element of the modern psychology of eating is what my elder son calls "the dog bowl mentality," a tendency to let the size of the container define the portion we expect to finish. And many of us have attended drinking parties where an analogous process—perhaps this one should be called "the punch bowl mentality"—generates expectations that guests should keep on drinking until the supply of grog is exhausted. It isn't just at fraternity parties where this punch bowl mentality becomes a race to the behavioral bottom.

My point here is neither to celebrate gluttony nor to deny the conspicuous virtues of moderation. The target is, instead, the silly romanticization of human nature. To say that moderate drinking is an unnatural act is not to disdain moderation but instead to respect the discipline that must contain our natural impulses with alcohol before moderation can happen.

And the fantasy of "human nature" as providing a healthy equilibrium for eating behavior is misleading and pernicious. This unscientifically romantic view of eating divides eaters into a normal group (the healthy) and abnormal subjects who suffer from defined pathologies, which are then labeled "eating disorders." The issue here is not the reality of specific eating pathologies at the psychic extremes of human behavior—anorexia, bulimia and epic over-eating abnormalities—as these account for a tiny fraction of truly serious eating problems in modern developed societies. The vast majority of us who eat too much, including most of us who eat much too much, are being pushed through the buffet line by the statistically and functionally normal psychology of eating. The way we are constructed and trained as modern citizens puts us at high vulnerability for overeating and its formidable array of negative effects. We have a problem that is if anything more difficult because it is an outgrowth of normal human instincts and psychology. Ditto excessive drinking. Thomas Hobbes turns out to have been a much better nutritionist than Jean-Jacques Rousseau.

The fundamental problems of eating and its effects are outgrowths of normal psychology and nutrition—and that is the essence of this essay's title—human nature turns out to be the most important eating disorder in the current circumstances of the developed world. The path to health is to cultivate an unnatural discipline. The sad, adult truth of the matter is that our "true self" becomes our natural enemy when approaching the desserts table.

LOVE AND FAMILY

5 • The Lifeboat as a Love Problem

6 • Looking for a Parking Space

7 • Love and Power

8 • From *The Wizard of Oz* to *E.T.* (by Way of Vietnam)

5
The Lifeboat as a Love Problem

The lifeboat quandary is one of those simple but intractable problems that make careers in parenting hazardous:

> *"You are in a lifeboat, Mom, with room for only one other person, and Timmy and I are both drowning. Who do you save?"*

The usual adult evasions of the issue do not survive eight-year-old scrutiny. "I'd get a bigger lifeboat" is quickly countered "But you can't!" The child's sense of fairness is offended by the attempt to give a pedestrian economic answer to a philosophical question. For similar reasons, "That will never happen" is regarded as unsatisfactory. The child's need to know his parent's heart is not founded on anxieties about the likelihood of a nautical accident.

What one friend of mine calls the Jewish Mother gambit—"I'd jump out and make room for both of you"—will also fail to satisfy the juvenile inquisitor. Either the rules forbid this sort of self-sacrifice, or Dad joins his children in the drink in the problem to make Mom's sacrifice insufficient to avoid hard choices. Needless to say, lame ducks like "You're both excellent swimmers" and "I'd never let you swim where it's dangerous" will be hooted out of consideration.

In posing the question, the eight year old in all of us is worried about love rather than water safety. He defines love as a competitive act of multiple choice. Three questions, which in other contexts have different meanings, here become the same: whom do you choose, whom do you love most, and whom do you really love? The question of whom do you choose becomes the only operational form of whom do you really love. And the architecture of the problem makes clear the central premise of this most arduous of life's examinations, choose only one.

Two elements of the lifeboat problem make it more troublesome for me than for some of my friends and colleagues: I don't think the problem can be solved by dismissing it as infantile, nor can the issue of singular choice be avoided by living a properly parsimonious emotional life. The lifeboat problem is childish in design, simplicity, and demand. That is one reason why there is so much to learn from it. But it is childish only in the sense that war, jealousy, ambition, and the feeling of uniqueness in the perspective of heaven are childlike qualities. These are also important emotions with pervasive effects on human behavior. The science of psychology may not be confined solely to the study of human immaturity, but that is certainly an important part.

And the lifeboat issue cannot be resolved by careful resource allocation. Having an only child certainly seems like a capital solution to the space problem encountered on the lifeboat. But in a world filled with spouses and relatives and friends, there are still problems associated with a lifeboat built only for two. When choose only one is the sine qua non of true love, when love is a zero-sum game, then ruthless jealousy becomes the state of nature. It is the definition of love rather than the size of the boat at the heart of the problem.

Most of us simultaneously live in the world of the lifeboat and fight it. I suspect that aspects of lifeboat psychology are biologically intrinsic. But coming to define love, as we all do, in a culture reeking of individualism and competition makes matters worse. This is clearest in our definition of romantic love, an Olympic competition for a gold medal that acknowledges no lesser awards. The demands for choice in romantic love are, we all learn, sadly legitimate. But the problem is broader. One does not need Sigmund Freud as a poster boy to know how very romantic a child's requirements are for a parent's love. Nor are these problems confined to biological circles. The strongest love of early adolescence is that of best friends, an evocative phrase for an intimate and intense same-sex relationship that demands rigorous loyalty that is the moral equivalent of monogamy as the only form of filial affection.

Similar impulses can influence the intimate relationships between employer and employee, mentor and protégé, teacher and student. As always, the language reveals: as in best friend, we must have a favorite aunt, or puppy, or rock star. Whom do you love? Choose only one.

We often seem to deal with lifeboat problems by adopting different definitions of love's limits at the sending and receiving positions. As parents, we compulsively sell a conception of affection that sounds like the miracle of the loaves and the fishes. We tell our children love is indivisible, so that what is given to one need not diminish another. We speak with great conviction of synergism at work, of the capacity to love as a muscle that once developed benefits all of its objects. "I love each of you the best" is standard parental fare, no less sincere for its apparent illogic.

Like supply side economics, this version of indivisible affection has both strong elements of truth and formidable limits. There is a capacity to love developed in its process that doubtless enhances love to come. There is also probably a tendency of tax cuts to serve as an incentive for further effort. But no government can run on the revenues from a zero tax rate. And despite the attractions of the emotional supply side, there are problems of priority in human relationship, undeniable scarcities of love that must be confronted.

It is when we are on the receiving end of love's expectations that we can feel the problems of priority with undeniable force. The child in all of us rebels at the notion of affection without election in any human setting where love is requested. Separating the appetite for love from the need to be individually special requires a transcendental leap, not out of our clothing but out of our skins. Can any of us do this? If not, is the capacity for authentic love inevitably a question of choosing only one?

There may be an almost satisfactory answer to the lifeboat problem, a solution that allows both love and survival, but it is not one that will comfort the young child who is a permanent part of each of us. The child's hunger will not be satisfactorily resolved because he or she is, as most of us are, allergic both to paradox and to notions of human limit.

The paradox of my lifeboat solution is that the awful responsibility of choice can be avoided because of our own mortal lack of power. The question "Whom do you save?" assumes that the salvation of another is possible. But to maintain a life support system through love and its sacrifices in the manner the question implies is usually beyond human capacity. Denied the power to resuscitate through love even once, we are spared the horrible choice that would accompany possessing such limited magic.

Our freedom to love widely and indivisibly is based on our incapacity to rescue in the course of love. Where there is human ability to rescue and support, love based on these functions is limited by the ability to live up to its implications. Then choices must be made. Nature planned well that humans have their young in small litters. But the natural limits on human power mean that we cannot protect any of those we love from life's ultimate hazard. Mom's correct answer to the lifeboat puzzle may well be "I can't rescue you or your brother, or myself for that matter. We will love each other very much, and sooner or later we will drown." If we cannot rescue, we need not choose. And love need not be competition.

This is the right answer for that very small part of us that is fully adult and for the adults that our children will become. For the child in us, love in the context of mortality remains a gyp. To love without the power to protect the object of that love seems a contradiction; but it is only a paradox. The children we give birth to will die. This is an element of life's logic, of love's topography, that is deeper than reason and as salient to meaningful modern life as anything.

6
Looking for a Parking Space

Those of us who live in urban neighborhoods and don't have private garage space are exposed each night to a peculiar lesson in priorities as we attempt to park our cars. At 6:45 pm, picking our way through traffic in the ten square blocks or so close to home, fifteen feet of legal curb space for the car seems one of the most important elements in life's quest. We experience mood swings, frequent frustration, aggression, and great relief when this temporary victory is won.

Then it's over. What fully occupied our attention at 6:45 pm, the high personal priority of the moment, becomes relatively unimportant at 7:02 pm because the problem is solved. And by 7:15 pm, when our significant other asks about the high and low points of the day, the search for parking will not be part of the news. The parking problem remains important only as long as it is unsolved. It is then not important until the next time, and many elements of our lives fit this cyclical pattern.

Under these circumstances, the significance of urban parking as a social problem obviously depends on when you ask. And the fluctuating significance of things like the parking place in our lives may clash with the need we have to view ourselves as psychologically constant people with a relatively stable sense of personal priority. Isn't the need to be constant threatened when that which was of consuming importance just ten minutes ago so quickly fades from visibility on the personal horizon? Yet isn't this a common feature of the drives that govern and enrich our lives?

We tend to accept the transitory importance of temporary conditions when dealing with physical drives that lack significant moral dimensions. The powerful influence of heat and cold, of thirst and hunger can be acknowledged without threatening our view of ourselves as psychologically constant. "I could have killed for a cold beer" is a statement uttered with equanimity by a person now no longer thirsty, and far from currently homicidal. This speaker feels no dissonance, no sense of two inconsistent selves, one thirsty and one not.

But when moral and emotional dimensions are involved, the psychological importance of temporary conditions troubles us more. Sexuality and anger, love sickness and the momentum of competitive drive, these are powerful emotions that transform our priorities until the moment and the need pass. These are also threats to the image of the constant self. We would not comfortably utter in public the equivalent of "I could have killed for a cold beer" about sexual need or loneliness.

And just who is the real me? The obsessed and excitable fellow looking for a parking space, or the placid and sanctimonious citizen well parked for the night? If both of these are aspects of my personality, which is the more authentic?

There is no logical or linguistic reason to assume that human behavior is governed by a single fixed set of preferences called a personality or self. There is, however, a powerful psychological and socially derived need we have to view our personality and character as constant. However much we might concede the variability of other people, there is an emotional drive to regard the person we carry through social life as one consistent personality. This need gets expressed in a variety of strategies that are intended to resolve conflict between driven and satiated selves by declaring only one version as authentic.

On the one hand, there is a series of what I would call anti-romantic arguments designed to persuade us that the preoccupied fellow cruising his neighborhood for a parking space is not an authentic version of himself. One argument against the driven self as authentic is that this version of personhood is less susceptible to control and therefore less real. The fallacy here relates to the conclusion that lack of control makes the driven self somehow less true. Why is that?

We can and should avoid making major life decisions while too hungry, angry, lonely, or tired. But not necessarily because these states are inauthentic expressions of feelings. Visiting the supermarket while ravenously hungry, while "out of control," is one way to distort one's choice of foods and grocery budget. But forgetting the extent of one's appetite or personal preferences in food while in the supermarket seems equally ludicrous. While hunting for a parking place, I may be willing to spend amounts for garage space at variance with later versions of my priorities. But deciding how much off-street parking accommodation is worth to the real me without considering my nightly effort and frustration is equally silly.

A second anti-romantic argument involves saying the driven self is not authentic because the influence of the drive is "only temporary." Pay little heed to the ardor of romantic love, we are sometimes told, because it will pass and leave a series of decisions in its wake that you will regret. This advice is a variation on not going grocery shopping on an empty stomach. You will buy more than you can afford and thus will regret your choices later when you are no longer hungry.

The problem here is twofold. First, many of life's hungers are temporary conditions only if we do something about them. Hunger and loneliness are two examples of conditions that may not pass if not attended to. Anger by contrast may dissipate with the passage of time. And the unmet longings at the soft liquid center of romantic love can seem as temporary as the 300-year-reign of the Ming Dynasty.

A second problem with downgrading the significance of drives because they are temporary is more fundamental: all emotions are temporary conditions. Logically, it makes as much sense to say that we are only hungry until we are full as it does to say that we are only full until we are hungry. Life is a temporary condition.

A final version of preferring the authenticity of the undriven version of the self is our tendency to place a higher value on that form because we regard it as morally superior. People who are not frantically searching for parking spaces are better, more courteous drivers. We should therefore construct our rules and regulations with this pattern of human personality, the truly reasonable person, as the model.

There is much to be said for designing rules for human interaction as if people were somewhat more reasonable in their behavior than is frequently the case. Yet imagining people as they should be is still no substitute for describing people as they are. Further, the rules we design for conduct may miss the mark if they do not account for our drives. They may not predict behavior. And they may obscure appropriate moral distinctions. Courteous driving at the height of the search for a parking place deserves special recognition on earth as well as in heaven. And much of the very finest of human behavior acquires that edge from the resistance to personal pressures that condition its commission. One must recognize the terrible pressure to find a parking space to properly value the courtesy of one would-be parker giving up a claim to a space in favor of another driver.

There are of course romantic fallacies as well as anti-romantic ones. The temporary condition of personality under passionate pressure is often viewed as the more real or more legitimate because of its high intensity. This judgment, too, contains a sneaky normative element, one that parallels the anti-romantic notion that the satiated self is more authentic because it's nicer. If intense is better than relaxed, then it might be better to be a person who is more intense for more of the time. But even if this is so, there is little evidence of a human capacity to successfully wish oneself into a state of permanent intensity. And could there be anything sadder that the spectacle of someone trying to transform themselves into a state of permanent hype, a sort of Hugh Hefner syndrome?

Individual personality itself is neither hungry nor full; an individual's character is a continual collaboration between various states. To take sides in the tug-of-war between the driven and satisfied versions of self is to miss the essential process that determines character. Why should we wish to do that?

The non-constancy of self is so obvious that our discomfort in confronting it merits attention. Moods are the most human things about us. They cover the world of experience so fully that no gift is greater than a good mood, no deficit more pervasive than its opposite. Of course, they vary. Why all the fuss?

I think we hope to maintain the illusion of control. To appreciate that personality has its cycles as well as seasons, that intensity and repose are fluctuations which condition human behavior, is to undermine the notion of the constant self as a controlling force. The moral responsibility of character under the influence of cycles of need is not only possible to understand, but also more interesting to consider than mechanical models of moral accountability. Lust, after all, becomes a foundation for meaningful virtue.

But to see the self as floating on changes in context and mood and biological need is to accept a rather modest account of the role of will in shaping individual needs and tastes. The dialectics that form us are not of our making. A moral life is achieved only by arbitrating the struggle within each of us. We cannot wish that struggle away.

7
Love and Power

What do we know about the distribution of interpersonal power in the following cases?

1. Bruce Springsteen is a rock singer on concert tour. Jane and Jim are two of a large number of fans who have not yet been able to get tickets for his concert.

2. Smith is the maître d' in a French Restaurant. Jones is a customer with a reservation who asks for a table by the window, tips Smith twenty dollars, and gets the table he requested.

3. John loves Mary, who might or might not love John.

The dimension of power illustrated by these examples is this: in each case one person is more important to another person than the second person is to the first. Although not the only way to think of power relations between people, this perspective provides one useful introduction into the dynamics of personal power. This aspect of power also deserves attention for what it reveals about the relationship between love and power.

A traditional sociological definition of power speaks of the ability to cause others to act, without explaining why this might be the case. Speaking of the importance of people to each other carries matters one small step further, without discussing the different reasons why people might attach significance to others. Bruce Springsteen has the ability to influence Jane and Jim because he is important to them. Jones may have power over the waiter if his twenty dollars is important. The waiter has power over Jones if he really wants that table.

Thus, the situation of a rock star and his fans is a clear case of power discrepancy. The circumstances involving the customer and the bistro maître d' are more ambiguous. And John, by loving Mary, is rendering himself powerless just as Mary may cede power over herself by loving John.

The rock star has power over his fan because he is much more important to each fan than each fan is to him. In a collective sense, a performer may need an audience more than the audience needs him. Musicians may spend more time and effort pleasing fans than an individual fan invests in pursuing or appreciating the musician. But even if the rock singer becomes prisoner of his fame, the power dynamics between him and any particular fan are clear. What he says or wants is more important to the fan than what the fan says or wants is to the singer. Bruce Springsteen will probably remember little of the conversation with a spectator in New Jersey, but the lucky spectator will remember the dialogue forever. That is power.

Interpersonal power is an important element of the exchange between the diner and the maître d' but the power relationship is more ambiguous than the rock star's relationship with his fan. The exchange of money illustrates rather than resolves the undefined power relationship. As in most social relationships, money counts. But we do not know from the exchange whether the table is more important to the customer than his twenty dollars is to the waiter. The customer could be a wealthy man with little need for money and only a marginal preference for tables by the window, or a man of modest means with a great need for a view on a special occasion.

If the table is important to the customer, the waiter has power in that context even if his customer is higher in social standing or has a great deal of money. But the power is limited to the setting in ways quite different from rock stars and many of their fans. Frequently, power is contextual in this sense. More "powerful" people in society all have anxious moments at the mercy of meter maids, traffic cops, people who teach their children, and hospital nurses.

* * *

What do we know about power when we say that John loves Mary? We know, in one significant dimension, that loving is the very opposite of holding power. Whatever else love means, and in all its manifestations, loving someone is conferring the importance of their life over yours. If power is being more important to another than he is to you, love moves in the reverse direction: it is simultaneously a gift of power to another person and, something different, the processes of becoming powerless oneself.

Viewing love this way illuminates some aspects of behavior and emotions in a world that contains both the impulse to love and the drive for power. Can we seek power over people and still voluntarily wish to cede power by loving others?

The little power broker in most of us will seek safe ways of loving, a concept no less attractive for its evident impossibility. We may try to restrict our love to settings where we do not compete for power, to love only those over whom we hold a great deal of countervailing power, or to love only those who love us in return. These tactics may limit the risk of giving power to the object of love. None of these maneuvers will cope with the larger problem of becoming powerless by loving.

One approach to resolving the tension between love and power is to keep separate the social spheres in which each is pursued, to seek love in the haven and power in the heartless world. This segmentation of self is a frequent part of the mythology of modern culture and not infrequently we explain our own behavior in these terms. We build a "nest" by participating in "the rat race," accumulate power in an outside world to share its fruits among the membership of an inner circle. But this strategy of separate spheres is defeated by the ambiguity of modern social arrangements as well as by elements of individual character.

Most of us do not spend our working lives as part of an army of occupation, nor would we wish to do so. The instinct to pursue affectionate relationships would spill over in almost all working environments and particularly so in settings that emphasize cooperation and long term continuity. We want to work in one big family and would be frustrated if so much of our lives were off limits to familiar relations. So much for the rat race.

Even more does the need for power permeate the spheres we reserve for loving. The need to feel important, and to have our way, is nowhere more important than among the people who are most important to us. For people who find joy and security in being significant to others, in the influence that comes with power, the instinct to pursue power in intimate relationships is ever present and often irresistible.

Holding power over those we love is also an insurance policy we often seek against the terrible vulnerability of loving. If it is dangerous to give power by loving, why not give it only to those over whom we hold power in other ways? Infants and small children, lovable in so many ways, depend on those who care for them. Part of their appeal as love objects is that dependency. Similar reasons may explain the appeal of domestic animals, servants, and objects of charity as targets for caring by those who might be threatened by extending love to peers. Even among adults, and especially in sexual intimacy, the dependent intimate, the infamous "little woman" of the domestic doll's house, was long considered a safer repository for love than more independent adults.

Among the many drawbacks of this strategy are these: the impulse both limits the people to whom love can be extended and warps intimate relationships in order to preserve power. There are wonderfully admirable people we cannot love because they are too adult. We must continue to subjugate those we choose to love on this basis to preserve the foundation on which intimacy was based, an emotional footbinding usually associated with relations between the sexes and between parent and child.

Further, love invested only where there is countervailing power over its objects is a substitute for trust rather than an expression of trust. Can we really love those we must control? However necessary this maneuver is felt to be, and, however frequent its occurrence, it is nobody's ideal.

The ideal solution, in every age, for the power imbalance of John loves Mary is for Mary to love John. And one of the many virtues of reciprocal love is a state of power equilibrium.

Unreciprocated love risks the corruption of unilateral power. In this sense, Lord Acton, when worrying that absolute power corrupts absolutely, was writing a volume of romantic advice. Mutual love as a power exchange corrects the imbalance. The process that produces this mutuality in the emotional legend of the race is neither bargaining nor fortuitous, but a process of shared trust that necessarily involves testing love's limits without strong countervailing power.

Mutual love carries all of the efficiencies of bilateral disarmament. It also carries the disadvantage of bilateral disarmament in a world where many others will remain armed. Earlier, I suggested that loving another was both a gift of power to the object of love and a process of becoming powerless. Mutual love redresses the balance between the immediate parties to the relationship, but leaves them both vulnerable, that is less powerful, in the conduct of their lives.

If I love my child, all the people who are important in his life hold power over me. No matter how well my son reciprocates my feelings, loving him renders me vulnerable to teachers, girlfriends, employers, and the fates that in determining his destiny will determine mine as well.

If my child returns love's complement, he makes his own happiness hostage to a university provost he has never heard of, a subcommittee of Congress, and the Internal Revenue Service. My well-being is threatened by the motorcycle traffic around his school; my child's good mood is at risk if I smoke or don't eat properly. We are, to that extent, rendered powerless by the process of being important to each other. And there is no insurance policy, nothing we can do, to undo this state of affairs.

Nor should we. There is a basic tension between the powerlessness of loving and the deeper reason many people pursue social power. If we seek power as ironclad protection against disappointment, love is bad strategy. But the larger forces in life are beyond any control that can be attained with social power. The vulnerability that loving generates teaches us only what is inevitably true. Of course the fates of those we love are beyond our control. Our own destiny is also unassurable. The lessons of love are, thus, the enemy not so much of power as of power's illusions.

8
From *The Wizard of Oz* to *E.T.* (by Way of Vietnam)

I am glad that film classics such as The Wizard of Oz *and* E.T. *are still widely viewed by families today. My essay, which was written a number of years ago soon after* E.T. *was released in the early 1980s, touches upon the topic of the war in Vietnam, which had ended only a few years before, and which left us questioning our assumptions on every front.*

When network television presented *The Wizard of Oz* and *E.T.* on two successive nights some years ago, our most pervasive mass medium provided dramatic evidence of how far American attitudes had traveled in the forty years between these two great children's films. While similar in many respects, these two classic films could not have been more different in the picture of adult society in the United States each projected to its audience of children. The earlier film represents the United States as a republic of sweetness and light; the later portrays an unhappy and lonely juggernaut. I think the difference reflects a change in adult attitudes toward social authority, a change that seems on balance to be healthy.

Both *The Wizard of Oz* and *E.T.* use the classic storyline for a fairy tale in which a child threatened by an evil and powerful adult forces rises to heroic proportions and overcomes the threat. But the way in which *The Wizard of Oz* contrives its threat to its heroine tells us much about the image of the adult world that the film's creators wish to convey to its youth audience. Dorothy, our heroine, may have a few unlovely adults in her family but she has to leave her real home in

Kansas and conjure up the Land of Oz out of a bad dream with its phony proprietor and wicked witch. The most serious adult threat against Dorothy appears only in her fevered hallucinations and she is returned to her bed in bucolic small town America when all her battles are won.

Elliot, the child hero of *E.T.*, doesn't have to travel very far to find uncaring, incompetent, and threatening adult figures. Just about every adult in *E.T.*'s version of Southern California seems either inconsequential or malevolent. Elliot's mother, a beleaguered single parent, is well meaning but helpless, which is the best that can be said for any of the adults on display. Most of the rest of the big people in this movie are far from nice.

A classic portrait of adult malevolence involves Elliot's experience of frog dissection day in his school biology classroom, a brilliant scene where the teacher is depicted as a large-voiced and headless body that paces menacingly up and down the aisles. We are provided with the child's perspective, hearing the threatening voice but never making eye contact with its source.

So while Dorothy had to leave her real world to find threatening adults, Elliot must instead discover his heroic love object visiting from another planet. Most of the children in his world are hateful, competitive, and shallow. All the social institutions we see in Elliot's world seem as uncaring as the biology classroom that serves as our introduction to the glories of public education. When his outer space visitor says "E.T. want to go home," we can hardly blame him. The Southern California-cum-Earth encountered by this extraterrestrial does not make space exploration from his planet appear a wise investment.

The only element the makers of *E.T.* could have added to widen the contrast between its portrait of adult society and the postcard picture of Kansas in *The Wizard of Oz* would have been if the adult authority figures had opened fire on their children. Is it any wonder then that psychiatrists associated with the Swedish Film Board recommended restricting access to the film on the grounds that it tended to show adult society in a bad light?

But is *E.T.*'s critique of American society really bad for children? And was a Nutrasweet portrait of Kansas society a necessary package for the story of *The Wizard of Oz*? The context in which such fairy tales are set tells us more about how adult society wishes to view itself than it does about a child's real view of the adult world. Kansas was portrayed as a positive adult society because that was the message that adult

America needed its children to hear after a bitter and divisive depression on the eve of a massive world war. With Hitler, Mussolini, and Stalin holding power, an upbeat view of adult authority must have seemed as necessary to project as it was hard to sustain in 1939.

By contrast, the whole of the *E.T.* plotline could be summarized by the bumper sticker that tells us to "Question Authority." This skepticism about the powers that be could happen in a successful mass-market movie only because American adults were ready to have their children hear that message. Why this change?

What I think led to changing tastes in the nature-of-adult-society tutorials that we design for our children's movies is the particular history of the *E.T.* generation's parents. The kids who first watched *E.T.* were the offspring of the sixties generation. The experience and mythology of Vietnam, of the civil rights movement, and of our national adventures with Watergate all seem consistent with learning that unmitigated trust in adult society should not be regarded as a survival skill.

But didn't this breed a cynicism in children about the adult world that produces disaffected dropouts? I think the answer here is no. The classic dimensions of the fairy tale story in *E.T.* deserve emphasis here, as does the character structure of Elliot, the child hero we come to love and admire. *E.T.* is the story of the triumph of heroic individual good over organized evil. Nothing cynical there. And Elliot, the character we root for and come to identify with, hungers not for power but for intimate affection and loyalty. *E.T.* is a love story.

The particular vices of the adult social structure under attack in *E.T.* are its emptiness of affection and support. The evil of the individual adults in this film is their willingness to violate trust. Many of the adults, like Elliot's mother, are themselves victims of loveless betrayal. E.T.'s bequest to Elliot is neither precious jewels nor godlike powers; his ultimate gift is the magic of his continued emotional presence in Elliot's life.

The competition between the human need for affectionate expression and the frustration of that impulse by organized society is the central theme of much romantic fiction. *Romeo and Juliet* clearly displays its own "Question Authority" bumper sticker. In this sense, *E.T.* comes from a much longer and more authentic romantic tradition than *The Wizard of Oz*.

Really, it is the All-American Agitprop of *The Wizard of Oz* that might usefully worry us. The terrible innocence of that film reminds us of one positive lesson that many have learned from Vietnam. We should distrust a society that needs to tell its children it will never harm them. Telling our children that adult society stands ready to facilitate all of their strongest and most authentic yearnings is truly the stuff of dangerous fairy tales. It turns out to be much better to motivate our children to make a better world than to teach them that the current model requires no improvement.

SUCCESS AND FAILURE AMERICAN STYLE

9 · What Was Portnoy's Real Complaint? And Why Should Hispanic and Asian Young People Care?

10 · Confessions of a Frequent Flier

11 · The Speaking Engagement as One-Night Stand

12 · Is Upward Mobility Just Another Pyramid Swindle?

13 · On Being Too Smart

14 · The Multiple Meanings of Money

9
What Was Portnoy's Real Complaint? And Why Should Hispanic and Asian Young People Care?

Almost five decades after its 1967 publication, Philip Roth's *Portnoy's Complaint* is regarded as a semi-retired cause célèbre in American letters, more important for its impact in its era than for any lessons it might teach in the twenty-first century. It is also remembered more as about sex and sexuality than as part of the distinctive Jewish American literature of the mid-twentieth century.

The popular recollection of the book misses both a central theme of the novel and with it the reason for the book's continued relevance to modern life. Portnoy's real complaint is about the psychic costs of achieving the success in the world his parents so desperately wish for him. Success in the world will require of Portnoy exile from the community, life style, and values of his family. Love and loyalty to his parents demand that this protagonist desert the people and places he loves for other places and priorities. And that ironic double edge continues to problematize the American dream.

My theory is presented in three installments. The first part examines the psychological portrait presented in the novel. The second part discusses the relationship between this type of family structure and upward mobility. The third section gives a rather optimistic prognosis for Portnoy's complaint, intended to reassure the protagonist and his millions of soul brothers.

I.

Portnoy's Complaint is a tantrum, a set of symptoms rather than a diagnosis. For my own limited purposes, four of the character's many parts are worthy of special mention:

- Alexander Portnoy, self-styled sex fiend, is really a superachiever and a superconformist at that. He is, at thirty-three, Assistant Commissioner of Human Opportunity in Mayor Lindsay's then-fashionable New York City government. He has been, in his words, first in every class he's been in, including law school. No matter how much he protests to the contrary, this is exactly the kind of achievement that both his father and mother revere. And this is not the only sense in which the protagonist is a good son. Never mind that it's never enough; he answers the phone, he visits, and he cares.

- Through Alexander's lens, the family is at once profoundly Jewish and at some distance from communal observance of the Jewish faith. The culture and community of Portnoy's youth is the Jewish-American semi-ghetto. The rules, rituals, and taboos are observed with a vengeance. But the Portnoy family is practically never observed going to services. Portnoy has a briefly mentioned bar mitzvah, his father attempts to round up the family once for Rosh Hashanah during Alexander's early adolescence and the local rabbi visits Mrs. Portnoy for "a whole half hour" prior to her hysterectomy. However, if Alexander's father regularly attends services, it has escaped his son's recollection. Instead, the world of Jake Portnoy is divided between a small desk in a Gentile-dominated insurance company and New Jersey slums where insurance is sold and premium remittances are unremittingly collected. Whatever religiosity exists resides within the Portnoy household, rather than the local congregation. One consequence of this is that rules, rituals, and constraints are handed down by Mrs. Portnoy, not Mr. Portnoy. The caveats of kosher life may or may not come from God, but God's messenger, his charge d'affaires in Alexander's household is Mom. This is in sharp contrast to the sexual politics of the Orthodox *shul*, where God's messengers and law-givers are male and authoritarian.

- Jake Portnoy is, in my view, the central character of Alexander's childhood and the central puzzle of the book. Heroically he squeezes out a middle-class livelihood for his family during the Great Depression. His physical stamina and perseverance are enormous. Yet Jake Portnoy is rendered by his son as ineffectual, constipated, and henpecked. He is at the same time the object of unqualified filial love:

> No money, no schooling, no language, no learning, curiosity without culture, drive without opportunity, experience without wisdom . . . How easily his inadequacies can move me to tears. As easily as they move me to anger!

The above quotation is typical but not fully disclosive. The fact that Daddy's grammar ain't too good is of some importance during Alexander's adolescence, but Portnoy's real anger is of earlier origin and deeper meaning: his father's failure to take a stand against the matriarchal preeminence of Sophie Portnoy:

> Pappy, why do we have to have such guilty deference to women, you and me—when we don't! We mustn't! Who should run the show, Pappy, is us!

You don't have to have a degree in psychiatry to surmise that in this particular family romance there was never an Oedipal struggle; rather, Alexander's father has lovingly surrendered, in advance, leaving a little boy thoroughly unprotected against the totalitarian bossiness of a mother only he can please, but even he can never please enough.

- One final element of the Portnoy family structure is both striking and demographically authentic: in the game of upward mobility, Sophie and Jake Portnoy have put all their eggs in one basket. There are only two children, only one is a boy. Alexander has no one to compete with for the glory or the obligation. Life is lonely, and very demanding, at the top. And this is exactly how things were (and are) in many upwardly mobile families. When the second generation of American Jews had kids, it almost seemed as if they had calculated college tuition in the bridal bed. And the same strategic investment in small families is currently used by many ethnic groups with strong ambitions for upward mobility.

All these things and more give us Alexander Portnoy, age thirty-three, full of guilt and achievement, eloquent, funny, immature—a dazzling combination of narcissism and empathy. He fears women, particularly Jewish women; he is concerned and ambivalent about his own sexuality. Such a man is in psychoanalysis for good reason. He is also, discounting Roth's hyperbole and difficulty with female characters, a remarkable and authentic post-mid-century Jewish-American achiever.

Portnoy struggles against what he sees as the ugly underside of the cultural values of his youth, but he recoils in horror from the "alternative lifestyles" of the Gentile world. He wants to be a man, a good Jew, and an American achiever. But how to wear three hats comfortably at the same time? Can a skeptic pray? Is lust compatible with Mrs. Portnoy's brand of Judaism? It often seems as if the protagonist regards such questions as the equivalent of asking whether elephants can fly. Alexander sees himself as doomed to spend an eternity out of his element: too Jewish for the Gentile world, too American for the secular communal socialism of Israel, too godless and sinful for the Jewish religion, and—most important—too good for Newark, New Jersey. Why should this be so? What is going to happen next?

II.

At the age of nine, our tortured hero imagines a Sunday afternoon in his adulthood; here are excerpts from one of the book's most eloquent passages. This boy's ambition for his adulthood is returning to Sunday dinner at one o'clock:

> . . . sweat socks pungent from twenty-one innings of softball . . . feeling great, a robust Jewish man now gloriously pooped —yes, home I head for resuscitation . . . and to whom? To my wife and my children, to a family of my own . . . my wife, Mrs. Alexander Portnoy, is setting the table in the dining room— will be having my mother and father as guests, they will be walking over any minute, as they do every Sunday. A future, see! A simple and satisfying future!

In his daydream, Alexander commutes from his own house in his old neighborhood to defend the poor and the oppressed in the nearby County Courthouse. As fantasies go, this is a modest one. Why then, doesn't this dream come true?

The answer is that Portnoy's dream is too modest. Alexander Portnoy identifies with the world of his father. But imagine graduating first in the class from Columbia Law School and announcing to these parents that "Mr. Big Shot," the family savior, is moving back to the old neighborhood to open a storefront law office in the ghetto. And not for a while, but for good. To say that Sophie Portnoy wouldn't approve is to put it mildly. But the real irony of this scenario is that Portnoy's father would regard such an act of loving identification as a betrayal. The last thing that Jake Portnoy wants is a son "just like me." The dialogue almost writes itself:

> For this you graduate Number One in your class? To handle two-bit cases in a grimy hole in the wall in Newark, New Jersey?

That Alexander's father sold insurance in the same neighborhoods, that he believed he was serving these people, is beside the point. The essence of Portnoy's childhood is mobility. Father, mother, sister, and protagonist are unanimous in aspiring to—indeed demanding—much, much more. To live the life of the big shot is to be exiled both from Newark, and from a life lived through paternal identification. On to Washington, on to the "Big Apple!" Honor your father by being somebody else!

What can the saga of Alexander Portnoy tell us about the psychic consequences of upward mobility in general? It seems plausible that whenever both parents want the son to be "much better" than his father, there is a potential threat to paternal authority and male model identification. (A comparable statement could be made, I suspect, when both parents support the proposition that a daughter must be "much better" than her mother, particularly earlier when "just housewives" were raising the next generation's liberated women.) To value the child's future status more than the parent's present one risks conveying the impression that the child is more important, more virtuous, and ultimately more obligated than the parent.

There are two corollary risks in the wish for upward mobility. First, high achievement requires high ambition. This entails one kind of cost when junior has to "live up to" a successful parent. It is also stressful when a child has to "live up to" his parent's dreams rather than their achievements. To inspire this sense of obligation and ambition requires, excuse the expression, "quite a noodge." Sophie Portnoy, even in Roth's shrill parody, is a conspicuous agent of upward mobility. Second, being "much better" frequently requires a form of exile in time, place, and role; upward mobility is a journey into the unfamiliar. In the sphere of emotional geography, the trip from Brooklyn to mid-Manhattan has been called one of the world's longest. From Newark, New Jersey, the trip is just as long and disorienting. It is easy to feel alienated and nearly impossible to retreat without denying the dream. Alexander Portnoy can be what his parents want for him, or he can live in Newark, but he can't do both.

The darker side of upward mobility is not confined to the Jewish-American family or identifiable ethnic enclosures. Just as one doesn't have to be Greek to have Oedipal problems, the dislocations and conflicts associated with ambitions for our children can be found in the careers of many families pursuing the American dream—Irish, Italian, Greek, Japanese, African American, Polish, and even just plain American. The tensions generated in families of upwardly mobile "outgroups" (such as African Americans and last generation's Jews) may make for easier entertainment, but the insight must be more general to be valid. You don't have to be Jewish to suffer from Portnoy's complaint.

To say all this is not to say that parental aspiration inevitably castrates fathers, deprives sons of paternal models, depends on Sophie Portnoy's memorable mouth, or sentences children to psychiatric consultation. Frequently, there are countervailing forces at work in a family that produce a more desirable equilibrium. The chauvinistic masculinity of Orthodox Judaism was one of such forces enhancing paternal authority. There are also many other kinds of family structure that produce successful children.

Finally, there is no law against fathers taking a stand in upwardly mobile families. Jake Portnoy's deference to maternal authority, his willingness to be kicked around by Alex through the course of his son's adolescence, and his failure to appreciate his own value are not inevitable concomitants of his son's later success. In identifying his son's welfare with his own subservience, the senior Portnoy may simply have been making a loving mistake. Alexander might have done rather well in law school even if his father had taken a stand.

But susceptibility to this kind of loving mistake is, I would argue, a regularly recurring feature of upwardly mobile families, and it is exacerbated by other regular features of that process. Small families facilitate educational and social mobility. They also put all their eggs in one or two baskets. Persistently high expectations generate anxiety as well as achievement. Doing it all "for the children" tends to produce the self-pity and self-congratulation that are the bread and chicken fat of Sophie Portnoy's existence. And doing it all for the children in a small, encapsulated nuclear family may be even more destructive when there is no countervailing force outside the family to keep things in perspective.

One such countervailing force is God, the God that Alexander Portnoy was raised without. This is a God who brings faith, authority, purpose, and reassurance. Rituals, rules, and constraints are not enough. When doing it all for the children is a family's only religion, it is both too much for every member of the family and profoundly not enough for anyone. Lacking both a God and a decent appreciation of their father, the Portnoys of this world have every right to seek psychiatric care.

III.

So how bad a disease is Portnoy's complaint? And what will become of our real-life Alexander Portnoys? On these questions I bear good news: Alexander Portnoy is moderately neurotic, immature, self-centered, and well on his way to growing up. He will continue to have problems "relating" to Jewish women, but this is a man on the verge of marriage, family, and psychosexual maturity.

The argument for this relatively rosy future is not without textual evidence, but Portnoy himself disagrees:

> Thirty-three and still googling and daydreaming about every girl who crosses her legs opposite him in the subway! . . . He lives in a condition that is neither diminished nor has in any significant way been refined from what it was when he was 15 years old.

This is the image of Portnoy that most readers and most critics recall. But these are the fears of the hypochondriac rather than his physician's diagnosis. In fact, Alexander is well on his way to sexual adulthood by the time he is twenty. The object of his developmentally appropriate college romance is one Kay Campbell, a thoroughly admirable and believable Antioch coed equipped with ideals, principles, and strength of character rarely seen in Philip Roth's women. The romance proceeds without interruption or sexual disloyalty for more than two and a half years. There is no evidence of "extreme sexual longings" nor the masturbatory marathons of Alex's early adolescence. The affair ends, as it probably should end, not because of Portnoy's lust or promiscuity, but because Kay Campbell will not convert to Judaism. Further, at twenty, our protagonist is not ready to be a good husband and father, but he's getting pretty close.

At thirty-three, he is awash with the longings that make husbands and fathers of most of us:

> Why then do I live by myself and have no children of my own? ... Professionally I'm going somewhere, granted, but privately—what have I got to show for myself? Children should be playing on this earth who look like me! ... Think of it, half the race is over, and I'm still standing here at the starting line.

This man sounds like good husband material. But if this is correct, what has taken him so long? How does the author take this nice, if stupendously spoiled, young man from the verge of adulthood and suspend his development for thirteen years, from age twenty to thirty?

He cheats, that's how. The entire decade of Alexander Portnoy's twenties is missing from this book and from his personal development. The only personal episode described during this period is a comic seduction of a New England country club type, who is portrayed in such gross caricature that even her second cousin wouldn't marry her. Fewer than ten pages of the 274-page book cover the entire developmental career of the protagonist from twenty to thirty. And the reason for this is simple: Portnoy never has his twenties. The character we're introduced to isn't really in his thirties; he is twenty-four or twenty-five, and just getting ready to sort out his neurotic ailments and settle down.

Whether his college girlfriend's successor is Jewish or Gentile is an open question. And Portnoy's adulthood will have plenty of social and emotional problems. But most of these problems—the relations between the sexes, coming to terms with the limits of upward mobility, and Jewish identity and its relation to the larger American culture—are the challenges faced by so many of his generation.

But children he'll have. And they in turn will have problems, "living up to" their father and creating their own delicate equilibrium in that fabulously complicated and promising world of Jewish-American modern.

But they won't suffer from Portnoy's complaint. The one set of problems a Manhattan-based next generation of the Portnoy clan will not encounter is the need to leave their roots in order to live up to parental ambitions.

So has Portnoy's complaint disappeared into the mists of twentieth century American history? Not quite. The need to reject one's origins in order to serve the ambitions that families embrace did not persist to the next generation of Jewish America, but it is sending the same painful mix of messages to the barrios and Chinatowns where the American dream of upward mobility currently animates family ambition. Today's Alexander Portnoy has a different surname, often Wong or

Gonzales. But the prospect of exile is still the ironic price that must be paid in the name of family love and loyalty.

10
Confessions of a Frequent Flier

Some time ago, the mail brought the news from XYZ Airlines that my thirty-odd-thousand miles of travel last year qualifies me for "premier" status in their Frequent Flier program. The details of my new preferredness are less important than my reaction to the honor: this was one of the most important, most positive letters of my week. I enjoy being a frequent flier—the paraphernalia, the prizes, the feeling of structure and meaning in an otherwise uncertain world. And I believe that exploring why these airline clubs became important to a large segment of the middle class can shed some light on modern American life.

The attraction of frequent flying clubs for me is symbolic as well as tangible. These programs combine elements of two great boyhood pastimes: Cub Scouts and pinball. Like Cub Scouts, the frequent flier clubs come with a language of their own, multiple layers of status to be awarded for achievement, special purpose insignia, and rituals. Every time the frequent flier reaches one pinnacle of hyperactivity, say 10,000 miles in a month, or 14,000 miles in a westerly direction, he is simultaneously congratulated and egged on to another goal that will differentiate him from his less peripatetic peers. Soon frequent flying will produce its own equivalent to the Eagle Scout, perhaps with a shoulder patch and a telegram from the airline president.

The allure of frequent flying also borrows from pinball. Enormous numbers are used to keep score in pinball points and frequent flier miles. These are probably the only activities in our daily life where most of us can score to the hundreds of thousands on a regular basis. To the extent that keeping score is important, and it must be, the feeling of achievement that comes from video games, pinball, and frequent flying owe something to the mystique of five- and six-digit numbers. We may not have Warren Buffet's bank balance, but we can measure our worth in large numbers.

Pinball and frequent flying also share what seems an ironic award schedule. The prize for playing pinball very well is the opportunity to play again on a cost-free basis, literally the hair of the dog that bit you. Such a reward structure does not fit with an instrumental view of the importance of pinball in life. For it must be the process of playing, rather than pinball as a means to an end, that attracts us if the prospect of more free games will serve as a significant attraction.

The reward, of course, for traveling so much is the opportunity to travel even more, only this time the jet lag is on the house. Travel is no longer a means to an end for many immersed in this system.

Yet the promised rewards of frequent flying are also seen as instrumental, a way of traveling away some of the imbalances that modern travel creates. Business travel, which we presumably do not enjoy, generates the entitlement for recreational travel. The airplane is, we hope, transformed into an instrument of pleasure. Solitary travel, which undermines family values, becomes the means to procure family travel. The frequent flier program thus provides a basis for elegant rationalization in which the most gruelingly mindless of business commutes can be described as premeditated hedonism and solitary business travel schedules are described as the road to family solidarity.

Widespread use of frequent flier clubs is also generating a new American ethic, a frequent flier machismo. Just as an earlier generation of men would feel diminished by having to pay for female companionship, paying cash money for recreational transportation is becoming a confession of status inadequacy. Paying for private air travel has become a secret shame.

The most disturbing aspect of the appeal of frequent flying as the way it responds to our neediness for meaning. The computer for XYZ Airlines knows more about my schedule than my family and friends. The monthly personal reminders I am mailed tell me that Zimring's trip to Washington last month and flight from Chicago week before last meant something in some cosmic scheme.

Often, this is the only palpable evidence that the trips we take, an increasingly large chunk of our lives, mean something to anybody. Only these programs tell us that there is a pattern that cumulates across the various flight segments of a modern life. This may be the only evidence we have that our travels fit coherently into a bigger picture.

As bigger pictures go, the cosmos of frequent flying is decidedly minor league. All the more reason the appeal merits serious study. With the decline of church and family, community and neighborhood, with the fungibility of executive work and the yuppified convergence of the professions into a single paper-pushing glob, upper-middle-class life has become an anomic roller coaster with the modern airport as its hub. How eerily fitting then that the computerized counting of our rings around this track, the rewarding of paid rides with free ones, becomes one expression of our individual hunger for meaning.

11
The Speaking Engagement as One-Night Stand

Most university professors greet the beginning of a term with a level of enthusiasm usually reserved for an outbreak of chronic disease. All professors think they teach too much, and any noncriminal means available to reduce our teaching load is greeted with joy. In a profession that already carries three months of annual vacation, the principal fringe benefit of the professorate is the sabbatical interlude when a whole year passes with no teaching. At well-regarded research universities, the tedium of regular undergraduate teaching is reinforced by the low social status of the enterprise. It is almost as if professors are allergic to the very activity that is supposed to form the core of their professional life.

But even the most burned-out denizen of the American professorate pines for the invitation to give a lecture at someone else's campus. The letter or phone call from a person we have never heard of at the College of William and Harry or the University of South Michigan is the bright spot of the week in which it arrives. Not only the trip to a new place, but even the lecture itself is an occasion for hopeful anticipation. Bored with our own colleagues, fed up with our students, we permit ourselves positive fantasies about colleagues as yet unmet and a roomful of other people's students. In such moments, hope springs eternal in a manner that is simultaneously sweet and pathetic. No matter how many times we have engaged in this scenario, no matter how dreary the outcome of most such adventures, many of us look forward to the next lecture at a new place with hope undiminished.

Why is that? What is there about the speaking engagement amongst strangers that quickens the blood? My thesis is that the speaking engagement is a legitimate form of short-term love affair that is irresistibly attractive in prospect. I do not mean to argue merely that one can draw an analogy between out-of-town speeches and short-term affairs; instead, I contend that the speaking engagement is one form of love affair, parallel in both structure and motive to the romantic tryst. Indeed, studying the contrast between lecturing one's own students and a night's work in another town may be one useful way of studying the appeal of other types of love affair as well.

The three great charms of the speaking engagement are the joy of being wanted, the promise of a fresh audience, and the prospect of short-term intimacy.

Just as the medium is frequently the message, one nice thing about the prospect of giving a speech somewhere else is the invitation itself. You don't get asked to make such a speech unless someone wants to hear what you have to say. This alone generates a wonderful feeling of being wanted that cannot be matched by professional colleagues who are stapled to you in compulsory relationships of tenure or by students who attend classes out of bureaucratic need rather than affection. Even more appealing to the fragile academic ego, the strangers who invite you to speak usually have developed an appetite to meet you by reading your published work. The academic writer finds no form of admiration quite as seductive as that based on a close reading of what he or she has written. So a large part of the allure of the outside speaking engagement is the feeling it conveys of being appreciated, of being wanted for all the right reasons.

Nor is high regard for one's published work the only reason we can anticipate being appreciated in a new city. An audience that has never heard our favorite jokes must be a blessing from heaven. The point is so obvious that its power is often underestimated. So often the "freshness" and "variety" we really wish is not so much new and different people to relate to as the sense that we ourselves are fresher and less predictable than our long-time companions may find us. That droll and dashing figure we can become performing before a new audience will experience a sense of renewal in self-image. That is exactly the sort of payoff that leads us to become frequent fliers.

The ideal outside speaking engagement resembles the paradigm of the one-night stand in one further respect: it is a self-encapsulating adventure that is highly significant to all the participants while it is happening but does not make large claims on our pattern of ordinary life after the fact. Usually, the half-life of the speaking engagement is over by the time the American Express bill is paid.

A large part of the emotional scenario of the visiting lecturer is that the people you meet there are suddenly and temporarily among the most important in your life. Over a period of twenty-four to forty-eight hours, you may eat four meals with your host, become intimately familiar with his career ambitions, and play with his children. But while the friendship and pleasant glow may carry on long after the visit, the intimacy is encapsulated in the time you have spent away from the environment of your everyday life and as a visitor in the lives of others. The experience can thus be costless and unthreatening, indeed almost euphoric, even as it is imbued with a sense of the temporary.

The academic speech as love affair, like its sexual counterpart, should not be hastily generalized into a long-term relationship. The University of South Michigan can only remain a place where people have never heard your jokes if you do not move there. The nice part of the temporary intimacy of the visit is that none of the ties and commitments of ordinary life need be compromised in the formation of the new and temporary bond. The short-term visit carries none of the costs of academic adultery or bigamy.

But all of this is easy to forget in the euphoria of the visiting lecture. And sure enough, in an eerie parallel to romantic courtship, academic recruitment for permanent positions begins with the short-term gratification of the visiting lecture. Awash in flattery, it is too easy for most of us to confuse the pleasures of the situation with the inherent virtues of the place. And this is a confusion that we seem only to learn about through experience.

To speak of the romance of the speaking engagement as temporary is not to say that it is either phony or lacking in importance. Many of the most wonderful things in life are temporary and some, like roses, derive much of their impact on our lives because of the shortness of their season. The speaking engagement can become a ceremony of refreshment for the visitor, as well as an opportunity for mutual intimacy that will enrich even a well-balanced life. As long as its limits are understood, here is one of life's rare harmless pleasures.

12
Is Upward Mobility Just Another Pyramid Swindle?

The American saga of Nelson Rockefeller was neatly summed up in the first paragraph of his *Washington Post* obituary:

> "Nelson A. Rockefeller was a vice president of the United States, a governor of New York and a multimillionaire noted for his generosity and his collections of modern and primitive art. The prize he valued most—the presidency of the United States—eluded him" (J. Y. Smith, *The Washington Post*, Jan. 28, 1979).

The paradox of Rockefeller's career was this: this man who served as governor of the nation's second largest state for 15 years, held prestigious and powerful posts under five presidents and ultimately became Vice President himself probably failed to measure up to own ambition—how does this happen?

For some people, the "all or nothing" ambition is a quirk of personality that is not clearly related to the dynamics of the larger society. Rockefeller's near-contemporary, Richard Nixon, was a man who had to be president or regard himself as a failure for reasons I cannot pretend to fathom. But in the case of Nelson Rockefeller, the details of his family history collaborated with the American ambition for upward mobility to make being Vice President of the world's most powerful nation seem like a painfully insufficient achievement.

Nelson Rockefeller was the grandson of the most successful capitalist in American history, John D. Rockefeller, who was probably in his time the richest man on the planet. Being the offspring and heir to John D. Rockefeller would certainly fall under the heading of good news, but it imposed a rather substantial drawback as well. The appetite for upward mobility from generation to generation is a major theme in American culture. In the litany of upward mobility, one important measure of a male is success in achieving more than one's ancestors. But if one of your ancestors is John D. Rockefeller, doing better than he did is a pretty tall order—there is not a lot of room to be had further up the ladder of achievement.

How then to stand out as special and worthy in the Rockefeller family album? If standing out is that important, perhaps the Vice Presidency won't do. And whether the pressure to reach for America's very top rung is implicit (as with the Rockefellers) or explicit (in the tyrannical passion of Papa Joe Kennedy), there are such extreme examples of all or nothing ambitions at the logical extremes of America's upward mobility.

But it is not merely the most extreme cases of the need for generational status improvement that threaten both emotional health and social harmony. If the target of striving for upward mobility is social distinction, that is to say moving up the ladder of status and relative achievement, it soon turns out that most of the objectives of the upwardly mobile can only be gained at the expense of other contestants. Much as we like to pretend that valuable achievements are not subject to inherent scarcity, for the most part they are. If everybody has a million dollars, then people with one million dollars aren't really rich for two reasons. In the first place, a mere million dollars won't buy many scarce commodities if everybody has that much to bid. In the second place, having a million dollars doesn't make the millionaire very special if everybody else has a million as well.

So the meaningful measures of progress in wealth, in professional status and in social standing are scarce resources, and the felt need the culture produces to do better than Dad (and now also Mom) creates a competitive race that relatively few contestants can win. Once we climb far up the distribution, the structure of a multi-generation upward mobility competition much resembles the classic pyramid scheme where each level of participant pays for entrance (to the people who are further up the pyramid) in the hopes of making his fortune from all the folks who will enter the scheme later and pay him for the privilege of recruiting others to this endless parade of riches.

The reason this is called a pyramid scheme is the shape of the distribution of customers who have to join for the payoffs to continue. If everybody on the top levels continues to make money with each new participant, lots more people have to join in each succeeding layer of the operation. If one has to double the size of each layer with each new tier to the financial scheme, then a tiny top tier can after a relatively short number of new levels require hundreds and thousands of new recruits to maintain its payout. From there it is a short trip from 100,000 (eight more layers) to 25.8 million. Four more layers after that would require more than the total population of the United States.

That's why pyramid schemes are doomed. The financial success of each new layer requires newer layers still. New customers are the only alternative to old customers coming up dry. So all pyramid schemes must eventually be failures, the infamous chain letters and many other variations alike, which is why they are called schemes or swindles.

And one ironic impact of the negative reputation of these schemes is that it's harder to find a large number of suckers unless the mechanism is designed to hide its character. What makes Mr. Ponzi invent stamp trading (and Bernard Madoff fabricate investment portfolios) is that these fantasies obscure the "sure to lose" character of the essential pyramid scheme.

The pyramid scheme and the need for upward mobility from generation to generation share two significant similarities and display one big difference. One key similarity between the mobility imperative and the pyramid scheme is that each game does produce some winners, and big winners at that. There is a Kennedy saga, after all, and millions of smaller victories in each and every American generation. And there are people who have prospered in the pyramid game as well, but not millions.

Yet the second important shared characteristic of the pyramid scheme and the mobility imperative is that sooner or later the inevitable consequences of continuing to play the game is disappointment. The more successful the parent, the more unlikely the prospects for the improved status of her offspring. In the aggregate, the system runs out of benefits to sustain it just like the pyramid. So there are winners and losers in both systems but the longer players stay in the game, the more likely they are to end up hurt.

The big contrast between the pyramid scheme and the mobility imperative is where the odds against success are the greatest. In each game, it is the earlier players who do best, but the early players in the pyramid scheme are at the top of the pyramid, while the early players in the mobility game are clustered at the bottom of their pyramid. And there is much more room for sons and daughters to do better than their parents at the bottom of the American social and economic distribution than closer to the top. So that the drive to be upwardly mobile works much better in those social and economic regions where it originated than up in the social stratosphere where Nelson Rockefeller was trying to out-achieve his grandfather.

Then why can't we only deploy the upward mobility imperative in those regions of the social structure where further mobility is not a fool's mission? The problem here is that the psychology of upward mobility is universally attractive. It turns out to be very difficult to restrict the impulse to want better for one's children, and for them to wish to rise further than their parents. There may be very little real room at the top in this eternal mobility competition, but the psychological urge to seek it is no less powerful because the odds are against success.

So is this one public competition where the rich pay more, where the cutthroat battle for prestigious nursery school slots is just the beginning of a lifelong process of regression toward the mean for the sons and daughters of privilege? Not quite. Money may not buy happiness and certainly can't guarantee upward mobility but it can provide plenty of resources to stave off downward mobility—good schools, connections, college board tutors, and orthodontia all shield our overprivileged kids from the specter of regression too far toward the mean.

But the more effective all these private resources are in giving advantages to the advantaged in competition for achievement in a new generation, the further the United States drifts from the imagined level playing field of personal achievement. Advantaged parents must cheat to create the chance that their kids can hold or improve their places. And even then, the failure rate will be relatively high.

Our current circumstances tiptoe close to the worst of both worlds, with intense concentrations of unfair advantage for high status kids who still face rather daunting odds against feeling successful. Wouldn't it be better to live in a culture that teaches most of its little Nelson Rockefellers that being very good is really good enough? Good luck to us all on selling that.

13
On Being Too Smart

A man I know has assembled a set of materials to teach graduate students about decision making. They involve the story of Robert McNamara, then the president of the Ford Motor Company, and the fiscally disastrous adventures of that company with the Edsel. Mr. McNamara was a super-achiever of unquestioned intelligence: World War II whiz kid, boy wonder president of the Ford Motor Company, United States Secretary of Defense for two presidents, President of the World Bank. Stunning intelligence, hard work, and high ambition made McNamara a wide-spectrum American success story over four decades. Yet the Edsel was one of two legendary mistakes associated with Robert McNamara in the judgment of history. The other was Vietnam. It is the juxtaposition of great ability and bad outcome in the story of McNamara and the Edsel that elevates the story from simple corporate comedy. That, too, is one tragic element of Vietnam.

There is one other element of the teaching materials about the Edsel of special importance to the topic I wish to pursue. These materials were prepared for a course offered to advanced students at the Yale Law School, an elite group who arrived at the school of their choice by a highly competitive process that validated their exceptional smartness. Most of them leave Yale certified for leadership positions in American life based on their intellectual gifts. Much to their credit, the materials raise an issue of special salience to this group: the occupational hazards, in modern American life, of being very smart.

Can there be such a thing as being too smart, and how might that be? We live in an age of information and analysis, if not an age of reason. Smart is rewarded and revered, particularly in the circles of influence and power that surround government and large-scale organizations. It hasn't happened yet, but a PhD might soon be a credential even for a major labor leader. It is already a status symbol for senior police officials.

Yet smartness carries risks, even when judged by the standards of a culture of rationality. The saga of Robert McNamara and the Edsel is not taught to the law students from the critical perspective of religious ideology or anti-rational pop psychology. One can also mount a critique of smart by smart's own standards, a list of social and psychological reasons of why very smart people might exercise power in unreasonable ways. Being hyper-smart may be a special case of hubris that is of particular importance in a world where high intelligence is one criterion we use to select those who make public choices. When we thus mix power and intelligence, problems may occur.

Here a few of the things that are hard for the hyper-smart: asking for help and accepting it; listening carefully to the non-super-smart; accepting the existence of insoluble problems and unanswerable questions; seeing the virtues of simple statements and solutions; and finding the right balance between humility and arrogance when both are necessary to the creative practice of smartness.

The interdependence of all in modern times is simultaneously a cliché and a profound truth. The more powerful our role in the social machine, the more we must and should depend on others. But the counter-cliché in American life is a romance of individualism that puts positive value on going it alone. And this is exacerbated for the super-smart by their own special competence at a variety of tasks. If my IQ is twenty points higher than that of a tax accountant, why should I pay him? Why indeed should I trust him? Yet here lies the path to isolation, disorganization, and underachievement, and this is not confined to issues of household management.

There is a general consensus that Jimmy Carter was much brighter intellectually than his successor as President of the United States, and it is also widely agreed that his go-it-alone brightness was one of the principal problems of his Presidency. What managerial lingo calls an inability to delegate is the dark side of the self-confidence that smart people need to operate. The tradition of self-trust is often mirrored with an inability to trust others.

Related to this, very smart people often have difficulty listening carefully to others who are not as smart as they are. A cult of smartness—and many institutions in American society approach that cult—gives little credibility to the opinions and views of those who are not similarly gifted. The problem here is that while there may be some positive correlation between IQ and wisdom, it is by no means complete. On our way to the Edsel, one problem with the decision environment in social institutions is not that of shooting the messenger, but simply not listening to the message because of the ascribed low status of its sender.

Hyper-smartness is also associated with difficulty in acknowledging those many problems in the world that do not yield to analytic solutions. If two persons, one much more intellectually gifted than the other, both face a problem that cannot be resolved analytically, it is by no means obvious that the more intelligent of the two will be the first to recognize that the problem cannot be solved. To practice smartness is often to believe in the intellectual solubility of problems; to acknowledge insolubility is to limit one's own strong suit. It is no coincidence that the man with a hammer is often the last to acknowledge problems that cannot be solved with nails. When combined with American optimism, self-confident smartness rarely admits to intractable problems.

When problems can be solved, there is sometimes also a tendency to disfavor simple solutions, solutions that are accessible to the not-so-smart, when they compete for approval with more complicated resolutions. For the super-smart, Occam's Razor has the disadvantage of letting too many cab drivers and BA's into the game. The complex and the paradoxical are by contrast the special province of the people with the esoteric equipment to reach them. My favorite published example of this phenomenon is the sustained attempt on the part of a political economist to prove that installing seatbelts in automobiles raises the accident rate. He almost certainly was not right, but one has to appreciate the extraordinary intelligence and theoretical mastery that are required to make this egregious mistake in credible fashion.

High intelligence is also a superb defense against learning the lessons of experience in relatively short order. My nominee for one of the most important lessons of Vietnam and Iraq was that intelligence and sophistication can postpone a confrontation with reality by multiplying the number of alternative explanations for observed facts. The longer it takes to learn many lessons, the higher the cost of tuition. The super-smart optimist, as much as the super-smart paranoid, can thus be an especially dangerous commodity in the world of policy analysis.

The next-to-last entry on my preliminary litany of impediments to brightness is less specific than some others, the tendency of self-conscious smartness to crowd out humility. Like many of the other potential flaws listed above, this is more a cultural and sociological phenomenon than a genetic drawback associated with high IQ. But to say that something is merely cultural in no way denies the seriousness of the problem or its intractability.

A final pitfall for the hyper-smart is the tendency to consider oneself expert in areas outside of one's special competence. This is a particular lawyer's vice in the United States, and it is therefore no surprise that I have endured more than one luncheon with law professors who specialize in estate and gift taxation but are possessed of no compunction about applying their gifts to foreign policy, race relations, or the mass media. It is all too easy for the gifted and spoiled to make the transition from being a quick study in their topics to instant expertise without any study at all.

Closely related to the problems of too smart are the hazards of being too witty and too creative. The basic problem of being too witty is a chronic incapacity to deprive the world of one's pithy insights. Some things should not be said out loud because they are not what is really meant, because they hurt people, or because the subject of the comment is none of the speaker's business. Many of us know that eerie feeling that the remark that one is about to make is better left unsaid. But what if it is really clever? The perfect putdown is no less hurtful and no closer to the truth because the phrase is beautifully turned. Yet the impulse to deliver oneself of the bon mot is almost irresistible. In this sense, the hyper-witty (who are usually also hyper-smart) frequently become the hostages of their own skills. Richard Russo's comic masterpiece, *Straight Man,* is organized around the consequences of the compulsion to let the witty observation fly.

In extreme cases, a career of wittiness can deprive the author of his other gifts. A talent for one-liners creates the impression in some practitioners that all the wisdom worth having can be compressed into aphorism. On many campuses I know, there is a senior professor, who was once of high promise, about whom it is said that he should have published his repartee.

Just as the renowned wit has a tendency to shower the world with his cleverness, the truly creative are apt to become compulsively innovative. In doing so, they fashion new approaches whether needed or not, and find themselves tempted to try things on the principle that if they do not, nobody else will. Creating the Frankenstein monster is thus the special occupational hazard of the creative mind.

With all these possible problems, it is still true that socially imposed control of the very smart is one of the world's worst ideas. Certainly our indulgence of some of the hyper-smart rewards immaturity and strokes egos to unmanageably outsized proportions. A tenured professorship in a major research institution much resembles a license to pout for many who are so blessed.

Yet any organized social response to the excesses of the gifted almost certainly does more harm than good. Good ideas, new ways of looking at the world, and new ways of saying things are in short enough supply. The chilling effect of outside discipline on smart guys and gals does more harm than good.

Not so the discipline of the self. My proposal, in metaphoric terms, is quite simple: a seminar in self-control should be a compulsory part of our curriculum for the gifted. Suppressing regard for intelligence is a bad social investment. But the combination of humility and high intelligence is what we most require of the publicly powerful. A society can afford to spoil its most gifted members only as long as they do not spoil themselves.

14
The Multiple Meanings of Money

One of the more remarkable things about the social science of economics is that it almost exclusively attempts to link the institution of money with theories of rationality in human behavior. My remarks here concern other than the rational assumptions of economics: the not so rational psychology of money. My thesis is that one way to gauge the distinct and non-duplicable identity of each human personality is to profile the numerous psychological quirks each of us brings to his or her relationship with money, to compose a psychological profile of the purse with no two profiles on earth exactly alike. In this sense, the profile of our financial peculiarities is what renders us distinctively individual—fiscal fingerprints if you will.

What follows is an attempt to set forth a few of my own financial fingerprints as a small down payment on a comprehensive psychology of money. For my introductory turn on the couch, let me nominate three fiscal quirks for public display: investment fever, male-pattern money/power syndrome, and my allergic diamond reaction.

Investments are Forever

Some time ago a close friend had the responsibility of making hotel room reservations for me for a week's stay in a foreign country. Knowing my love of ocean views, he reserved a room with a view despite the $15 nightly differential, a preference I reversed upon my arrival, saving $100 and mildly puzzling my friend.

The puzzle was this: at the time of this adventure, I was starting a search to purchase a house in the San Francisco area, where a panoramic view of the bay is a highly desirable aspect of real estate that is reflected in its cost. In looking to buy a house, I would not consider anything without a bay view, despite a differential of many thousands of dollars. Why the inconsistency then, my friend wondered, the sudden attack of terminal cheapness, when less than $100 separates me from a week of my life with an ocean view? Because the $100 was spending money, a personal taboo, and spending the many thousands of dollars to buy a house with a view was merely "investing" money.

For a person happy to spend the money, to say that cars, couches, or compact disc players are poor investments misses the point profoundly. They are not investments at all but items of consumption. Nobody objects, after all, to buying a magazine or a sirloin steak because one will not be selling it for a profit.

Nonetheless, basic differences in psychology separate those who comfortably spend large chunks of money on present pleasures and those of us who recoil in horror from purchasing a commodity, like a fancy car, that would immediately be redeemable in the market for far less than its purchase price.

The distinctions between spending and investing may seem wholly rational, the strategic consequence of thrifty values, but this rational explanation fails to account for the intensity of the emotional distinction between spending and investing, and for the many examples of lavish consumption that people like me can successfully disguise as investing. If the major psychological principle at work here were only the investment ethic, would the negative emotional reaction to spending be as pronounced, or as fearful, as many of us experience?

What is involved here for those of us who hate to spend can be seen as more of a hedge against mortality than any protection against currency depreciation. Long ago, my mother explained her reluctance to spend large amounts of money during her seventies as the fear that she would reach age ninety insufficiently provided for. The story bears retelling because I believe what she expressed as a worry was really a hope that if her money lasted until she was ninety, she would too. For many of us, spending money for consumption is a metaphor for mortality, a concession that our substance need not be hoarded over a budgeting period that extends to eternity. Some of the lure of investment is the siren song of immortality. Subconsciously, many of us hope that we will last as long as the positive cash flow.

The pejorative link between consumption and mortality is deeply embedded in folklore. What makes the famous tale of the grasshopper and the ant admonitory is the implicit message. The contrast to the grasshopper's spend-now-pay-later plight is the premise that the grasshopper will die and the thrifty ants will live forever. The enduring resort to the slogan "you can't take it with you" owes much to the persistence of our irrational belief that you do not have to go in the first place if you keep enough of "it" around.

For many, then, the link between consumption and mortality is a major deterrent to spending. Obviously, wealth will flow to those who will find ways to cater to our neuroses by disguising spending as investment. This subterfuge partially explains the appeal of the sale of tangible goods as a hedge against inflation. We are able to buy cabin cruisers and Persian carpets and say we are investing. This strategy is also brilliantly revealed in the advertising slogan that formed the basis for the title of this section. What, after all, is the psychological importance of the fact that "diamonds are forever" if we are not? Or does this advertisement promise a measure of eternity to us if our material means do not diminish. Perhaps we can last as long as our diamonds.

Don't Tread on Me!

What the police call "altercations" about money, along with arguments about liquor and sex, are listed as the principal cause of thousands of homicides every year in the United States. This statistic is simultaneously true and misleading, for the same reason that what are called arguments about money are a leading complaint that surfaces when couples are involved in marriage counseling and divorce. The point, no less important for its obviousness, is the link between money and power. Money is the surface topic; money issues are the medium over which power conflicts are fought in this culture, rather often between men and women.

To say that money is the medium for power struggles of this kind is not the equivalent of saying that it is *merely* the medium for conflict. But we often risk confusing the medium and the deeper message.

The scarce resource that animates most of our nastiest arguments about money is interpersonal power. Money in this culture is so often the measure of who wins, who is right, and who is important, that money and power are often viewed as the same. Thus, if married couples are having difficulties that they define as money problems, that does not mean that the infusion of cash would resolve those problems. Similarly, the kind of money argument that leads to homicide in bars or bedrooms will probably not respond to increases in the minimum wage or more generous programs of food stamps.

This link between money and power deserves special mention here for its capacity to explain the neurotic quirk that many of us, mostly men, experience as horror of being fooled in the marketplace. Why is there something that feels empty and invalidated in us when we pass a supermarket advertising Diet Pepsi at 30 cents less a six-pack than we have recently paid? Why will the same businessman who lavishly tips the waiter $15 also meticulously add every sum on the check to correct small differences before leaving that tip? Why the elaborate ritual, the deadly serious dance between the male prospective customer and the car salesman?

The terrible fear is of being bested, that's why. The businessman leaves the tip as an act of voluntary largesse, but his response to being at the mercy, even a dollar's worth of mercy, of the waiter would be rage. Being beaten out of a dollar or one thousand dollars or even thirty cents represents a diminishment of my intelligence or resolve or potency. It leaves us thinking less of ourselves.

This male-pattern vulnerability creates the opportunity for ingenious selling. To convince the customer that the purchase is actually a demonstration of his power is a giant step toward making the sale. Buying high priced goods that everybody knows to be expensive is a demonstration that the purchaser has the power to do so, and this is no small spur to the engine of conspicuous consumption. The appeal of confidence games is more than monetary greed: the sucker or mark is promised a great reward but the appeal of something-for-almost-nothing is more accurately an appeal to cupidity rather than mere desire, with rewards based on winning the game or besting one's neighbor, just as much as on spending the proceeds.

Any sales ploy that can create the impression of the seller's vulnerability is good for business. Here perhaps is the explanation of why business establishments merchandise their own failure, famously, in the "going out of business" sale.

The seller's display of vulnerability can be an important sales tool because, as with the confidence game, it excites the appetite of potential customers to exploit. More frequently, I suspect, the seller's show of vulnerability is a necessary precondition for the potential buyer to discard his own fear of being bested in the power game. As long as every seller is regarded as a potential adversary in a power struggle, the phrase "it's only money" cannot accurately describe the psychological dynamic to the potential customer. One of the major tasks of modern merchandising is getting the customer to that point where he thinks what he is about to give up is in fact only money. Needless to say, the homicide statistics and matrimonial complaints that were mentioned at the beginning of this section involved combatants who have not reached this plane.

The Trouble with Diamonds

Why am I much more likely to spend money on old French taxicabs rather than Porsches or Cadillacs, on rubies instead of diamonds, and on Paul Klee lithographs instead of Picassos? Because I have a terrible need to make a personal difference. And that ego need, quite consistent with lusting after the things that money can buy, still predisposes me against putting a high value on the things that any fool with enough money can find his way to purchase.

For me, the big problem with buying a two-carat diamond is that it is suitable for any occasion. Its preciousness and specialness are entirely conferred by the general culture in a way that makes it the obvious choice for a gift of precious jewelry. I find that profoundly threatening.

The threat is that all one needs to buy a diamond is large amounts of money and a sense of the obvious. For the woman who really wants a diamond, the only sense in which my specialness is important is the extent to which I am able and willing to spend money. In terms of my needs to make a difference as an individual, such a gift ranks imperceptibly higher than sending a large check. If, however, the principal criterion for my self-worth were the amount of money I could spend, there would be nothing difficult about a woman who likes diamonds. But my appetite for specialness requires a vindication of my personal taste as part of the romance of major purchase.

This leads to a need to champion less-popular causes, to march to a different drummer. This should not be confused with an antimaterialistic stance. Those determined to set trends in the material world, and so vindicate their personal tastes, end up spending more time and possibly more money on the getting of goods than their less ego-driven peers. Nor is it proper to think of those who follow the crowds as suckers and the self-defined avant-garde as somehow fiscally sane. The reverse can be true. The discovery of new artists can be a very expensive hobby indeed. And as for following the crowd, if you are clustered toward the front of the pack, it can be a wonderful investment strategy.

Moreover, the need to pioneer a new path of consumption renders one just as ultimately pathetic as the hot pursuit of majoritarian baubles. Needing to impress a woman with aquamarines can be every bit as sad as feeling romantically unarmed without the blessing of the DeBeer's diamond trust. And that may lead to one of the larger lessons regarding the pocketbook as a window into the soul. The wise anthropologist knows that all tribes are primitive, including one's own. There is something undeniably pathetic about the ways in which each of us expresses the need to be individually special.

This is, however, an insight that should produce tolerance rather than melancholy. How much less interesting the world, how much more barren our place in it, if money stood only for itself.

ORIGINS AND INFLUENCE

15 • As the Twig is Bent . . .

16 • On Being a Type

17 • Southern California as Roots

18 • The Exception that Proves the Rule

19 • The Arrogance of Nostalgia

15
As the Twig is Bent...

I like to think of this as a tale of two California rose gardens, separated by five hundred miles and forty years but otherwise closely linked by family influence.

Rose garden number one was installed in the back yard of the first new house my parents ever build from scratch, in the foothills of Studio City, California, in the early 1950s; this was the fourth house acquired during their marriage but the first time that they were masters of what this new suburban citadel would contain. And one significant chunk of our ample Southern California back yard became a rose garden, a collection of fifteen or twenty rose bushes of various different colors that, while not rare in Los Angeles gardening circles, were not all that common either. These were not front yard roses for public display but the back yard species designed for private pleasure. My mother liked roses, although where she acquired this taste was never made clear to me and her reasons for planting a rose garden were not an important subject of conversation or wonder.

And certainly the Zimring family rose garden was of no existential importance at all to the eight-year-old boy who joined his family's short migration from Hollywood to the San Fernando Valley. What flowers might be blooming in the family's new back yard could not have been of less importance to the Studio City sapling I was, let alone the middle-aged Berkeley law professor I became some four decades later.

And yet, when a house and garden were acquired in Northern California in the 1990s, it came with an elevated patch of lawn that was both impossible to maintain and ludicrously indecorous. Here, four decades after that first rose garden came the first genuine opportunity to choose my own garden. What to plant in the elevated rectangle of my Kensington dream house?

You guessed it, of course. Here was the second coming of the Zimring rose garden. Even though that first garden had never struck me as important, the precedent was quietly compelling when half a lifetime later my own floral ambitions were consulted.

And the pattern of repetition that produced my 1990s rose garden is not merely common in modern life but almost universal. Just as whole societies and social groups reproduce patterns of behavior and preference with customs, families and what sociologists call "subcultures" produce distinctive patterns of repetition. At the social level, we all expect and accept this—of course Americans drink coffee and the British drink tea; indeed, without such predictable customary patterns travel agents would go out of business. And the distinctive fingerprints of family background are all over every one of us. The sons and daughters of CPAs take up accountancy, football fans beget succeeding generations of football fans, and many more of the offspring of cigarette smokers become smokers themselves. These patterns are so ubiquitous that it is difficult to believe they are even interesting. What after all should interest anybody else about Frank Zimring's rose garden? And so what if the British drink tea?

There are three elements in the tale of two rose gardens that deserve attention. For one thing, the nature of the transmission of habits by example is subtle and not visible. There is no such thing as a rose garden gene to explain my devotion to flowers with thorns. We are dealing here with the software of inheritance rather than its hardware. What does the example of parental choice communicate to offspring? There may be both informational and normative messages that parental examples communicate. One thing that nine-year-olds learn when their parents plant roses is that roses can be used for decoration and display—here is one thing one can do with back yards. Let's call this example as precedent. When confronted later with the back yards of adulthood, the previous experience reminds us that roses are possible. There is a normative flavor as well to the memory. Parents planted roses because they thought roses were pretty, were the best flowers to plant in a garden, and this is the parental example as a preference, a message about the quality or status or pleasure of roses.

The predictive power of normative and informational parental cues is substantial for most of us, but neither visibly dominant nor inevitable. I cannot imagine that roses struck the nine-year-old that observed his first rose garden as important or a foundation for any ambitions about adulthood. There were a lot of things I thought I wanted to grow up to be in 1953, but a planter of rose gardens wasn't one of them. Nor were roses or any other decorative plants ever on my radar screen during the Johnson, Nixon, Carter, or Reagan administrations. So any affection I may have carried for roses was a latent element for much of my adulthood. A set of impressions that did not seem of great importance at the outset can still end up determining preferences after a delay of forty years. Why is that?

The power of parental example is by no means inevitable. There are some children of lawyers who would rather join the French Foreign Legion than the family firm, and while accountants sire more than their share of CPAs, many of their children have other ambitions and values. And the influence of parental example will often weaken in the face of widespread social change. Even though the children of smokers are much more likely than others to become smokers, such offspring are much less likely to smoke than their parents since both the rate of smoking and its social standing has diminished. The transmission of racist attitudes fits the same pattern of decline over time as cigarette addiction. The children of the racially prejudiced are more likely to be prejudiced themselves, but the prevalence of prejudice declines over the generations as racism falls out of fashion.

Part of the pattern that made me into a middle-aged rose gardener was the simple transmission of values that inclines us to admire the things we were taught to admire. But beneath the surface of this, and separately important, our parents provide our first and most powerful lesson about what adults do and are in the world. We witness the adult choices of our parents and store those memories for the time when we confront similar choices as adults. It is then that the remembered example of adulthood observed becomes powerfully relevant to our adult lives. These were the first adults, the first men and women, the first husbands and wives we had ever known.

As the twig is bent, in this account, so grows the tree—but only if you wait long enough. And as much as Sigmund Freud is currently out of fashion, his understanding of the power of example has stood the test of time.

16
On Being a Type

In the movie *Annie Hall*, the following exchange takes place when the Woody Allen protagonist, Alvy Singer, first meets his wife-to-be, Allison Porchnik, at a 1956 political benefit:

Alvy: *You working for Stevenson all the time or what?*

Allison: *No, no, I'm in the midst of doing my thesis.*

Alvy: *On what?*

Allison: *Political commitment in Twentieth Century literature.*

Alvy: *You're like New York Jewish left-wing liberal intellectual, Central Park West, Brandeis University, socialist summer camps, and, uh, father with the Ben Shahn drawings, right? And, you're really, you know, strike oriented, kind of . . . uh, stop me before I make a complete imbecile of myself.*

Allison: *No, no. That was wonderful. I love being reduced to a cultural stereotype.*

About this dialogue we can ask one of the world's easiest multiple choice questions: Is he putting her down or courting her? The answer is "all of the above." Our hero is accusing this nice young lady of being a type, but his description is obviously of just the kind of type he values most highly. Allison's reaction reflects the ambivalence we all feel toward being typecast, which is why so many find this passage from *Annie Hall* evocative.

The way in which most of us relate to being seen as a member of a particular culture, that is to say being a "type," fairly radiates ambivalence. We typecast those around us all of the time. We typecast ourselves rather frequently and without adverse reaction. But to be described as a type by others, even in the same terms we might use ourselves, carries negative freight.

Thus, the same Allison Porchnik who half resented "being reduced to a cultural stereotype" would probably place an ad in the personals column of the *New York Review of Books* describing herself something like this:

> "Divorced Jewish female, liberal, intellectual, with strong interests in literature and political commitment . . . ."

Why the insult, then, when someone else accurately describes her major affiliations, styles, and interests?

The answer to this puzzle is an important piece of Americana. The Allison Porchnik in all of us believes in identification and in belonging. We wear the class rings of Brandeis or Florida State with pride. In adulthood we prefer our parents to other people's parents. We value our children more highly than any other life on Earth. But we resist seeing ourselves as determined by forces outside of our control.

Typecasting ourselves is a voluntary act, and thus consistent with the myth of self-invention each of us treasures. Being typecast by others feels like being poured into molds that seem beyond our control. As long as I am doing the describing, I can think myself capable of being any type I might wish. But the same description of me by another person will seem imposed, determined, unfree.

This tension between being typecast and the myth of self-invention is a powerful explanation for the particular resistance in American culture to typecasting. In traditional societies, where the need to be self-invented is less strongly felt, the resistance to being a type will be much lower. In most of the world's stable societies, to become a chip off the old block is regarded as a noble aspiration. In the United States, where nine out of ten high school senior boys say they do not want the same job their father has, being a chip off the old block may seem like unattractive typecasting.

The special concern of Jews with matters of types and typecasting has one obvious explanation but perhaps another subtle one as well. First, the obvious: stereotypes of Jews and Jewishness imposed by others are literally a life and death matter. In many places around the world, once a person's Jewishness has been described nothing else about him has any significance. The imposed stereotype thus threatens both individual and group freedom amongst Jews with special force.

There is, however, a second reason why Jews who exist in most places as a cultural minority tend to focus attention on types and typecasting even without the threat of negative stereotypes. Minority status itself generates special sensitivity to differences between groups.

A native of a remote South Seas Island who lives all his life amongst members of his tribe never thinks of himself as a type. He is the only sort of person he knows. The way he paints pictures or wears his hair or worships a deity seems to him an aspect of the human condition rather than the trait of a particular group. Similarly, in homogeneous societies somewhat closer to home, the question of type never occurs if everyone a person knows well is the same type.

And when majority and minority cultures coexist, it is the minority that will be thought of and will think of itself as adhering to a distinctive type. If ninety percent of the population dresses one way, it is the ten percent that does not who will be thought of as different, and may think of itself in these terms. It is the habits of dress of the ten percent that will make its members into types.

Perhaps this happens only when the majority is socially dominant as well, but most majorities outside of South Africa are dominant. Prior to Israel, Jews always lived with majority host cultures that were socially dominant, *The Protocols of the Elders of Zion* to the contrary notwithstanding. From the feelings of being different and set apart in such a setting grows concern about being a type.

The irony here is that one must see oneself as different from others before conformity to type is put at issue. It is that sense of difference from others that helps make so many American Jews into students of social type. The most determined conformists, those who never deviate from running true to type, will never examine the patterns that determine their lives. For the most part, it is those who have taken steps toward independent awareness of their lives who worry about being a type.

17
Southern California as Roots

On a recent business trip to the city of my birth, I experienced what can only be called the shock of recognition. Emerging from a television studio in a venerable section of Hollywood, I encountered the old Nickodell Restaurant, a landmark of my youth, as well as the scene of a sophisticated, yet affordable, youthful birthday dinner.

This restaurant encounter is the stuff of nostalgia, but why a shock of recognition? Two reasons. What I saw was not a restaurant from the same chain, or even one with the same name, but the very same restaurant still operating in a very different world. And encountering a still-functioning institution of my youth is as singular as the feel of shaking the paw of a living mastodon because the city of my birth is Los Angeles.

Back before the whole world abutted a shopping mall, Southern California was a preview of coming attractions, of the metropolis as roadside stand. Those of us who grew up in this theme park of the modern can consider ourselves the sons and daughters of a new American revolution. We are veterans of a social organization that did not engulf the rest of America with its suburban sprawl until the 1970s. What can this experience teach about the sense of origin that will be experienced by so many of the young who "come from" shopping mall America when it is their turn to search for and identify with their roots?

Here are three things that seem different about the search for roots in Southern California: the scarcity of manmade landmarks, the displacement of nostalgia, and the absence of any status quo as a reference point.

One singular element of the Los Angeles of my youth is that there is not all that much of it left. The manmade public institutions I remember are largely displaced. Many of the buildings that were the public infrastructure of a metropolis of two million are gone. In this sense, the nostalgic's guide to the Los Angeles of the 1950s is one of the world's shortest books. And even some places that have the same labels as the institutions of my youth have metastasized beyond recognition. Knott's Berry Farm is in any event a poor candidate for creeping nostalgia, but the place called Knott's Berry Farm today does not even resemble itself in former decades.

All over the megalopolis, many of the buildings and institutions of my youth are buried under two and three layers of succeeding physical civilization. And there seems no orderly progression to the burial of the physical world of earlier years. The so-called "Zonal Hypothesis" of urban development in which newness spreads in succeeding outward rings from the core of the city does not appear to be a dominant mode in Los Angeles. Nor is the pattern one of classic urban renewal, where the very oldest parts of the central city are most exposed to the wrecker's ball. Paradoxically, much of what seems to have been least protected from physical change include many of the most modern elements of Los Angeles in the 1950s. There is less evidence in many parts of Southern California of the 1950s than of earlier eras.

Southern California thus seems a dramatic illustration of the short half-life of the modern, with the new soon covered by the newer still. One consequence of this is that most physical landmarks that seem historic now in Southern California are those that seemed historic in 1955: the Santa Monica fishing pier, the Hollywood Bowl, the Los Angeles Coliseum, the Greek Theater. The only manmade landmark to have emerged from my youth is Disneyland.

Much of the reason why the Southern California new is displaced by the newer is related to economics and transportation. But there is also a psychological aspect worthy of mention. What was so recently modern, what was justified in relation to its modernity, cannot appeal to an ethic of preservation in its defense. It is thus the new that is particularly undefended against the assault of the newer still. The old Hollywood of my youth is represented by many landmarks, it has an ecological texture of some familiarity. But the public world of Sherman Oaks circa 1958, indeed circa 1968, seems gone forever.

If the physical locations of one's childhood and adolescence disappear, what becomes the basis for the attachments that comprise the sense of one's particular origin? What is it that one has the sense of being from when one is from Southern California? For starters, those few physical landmarks that remain evoke strong feelings. But there is also a displacement from buildings and physical institutions to other aspects, to intangibles, to movable property, and to nature. If the corner drugstore is gone, we attach particular significance to the styles and music of its now-departed soda fountain. If the house next door is buried under a succeeding freeway, a '57 Chevy like the one that used to reside in its driveway becomes the vehicle of special nostalgia.

Perhaps more important, there may also be the seeds of ecological consciousness in the impermanence of Los Angeles architecture and buildings. One thing that is still the same about Santa Monica is the Pacific Ocean. The fields and trees and beaches and valleys remain; juxtaposed against the impermanence of the manmade environment; these natural monuments play a larger role in our sense of place. In this sense, being a child of the shopping mall culture gives one a head start on environmental consciousness. One way to understand the importance of what can be permanent is to grow up with a strong sense of the transitory nature of almost everything else.

And it is not just buildings that are constantly ground under by the processes of Southern California. Change and mobility have been the secular religion of Southern California in every era of its rapid development. For this reason, the Southern California nostalgic can be a reactionary or a revolutionary, but never truly a conservative. There is nothing to conserve. Harking back to the good old days of a Southern California childhood is to idealize a scene that was itself constantly changing, that had no fixed identity. The status quo of Southern California was always a moving target.

One popular way to adjust to this fact is to deny it. It is no accident that Southern California was always a fertile ground for static fundamentalism in religion, politics, and social prescription. But unlike the fundamentalist movements in the South and Midwest, the hunger for an unchanging social order in Southern California was rooted in no contemporary or historic reality. For most of Southern California, for most of this century, Elmtown and Main Street had the same degree of reality as Shangri-La as models of social organization.

There may be advantages to growing up in an environment of perpetual change. A certain amount of flexibility becomes a survival characteristic if one is from Southern California, just as the freeway system is a Darwinian spawning ground of good drivers. And growing up in an atmosphere of constant change teaches the limits of change as a solution to current problems in the clinic of the real. If the Southern California nostalgic cannot be a true conservative, he or she can become both cautious and worldly at an early age.

And just as the values of the environmentalist are enhanced by learning how fragile the ecosystem really is, a survivor of Southern California knows better than most how much the social institutions around him or her are creatures of contemporary human effort and current need. The children who grew up in the Southern California of my youth are on notice that social conservation is our job. All this is of special importance in the United States of the twenty-first century. Almost wherever we live, our children are all from Southern California.

18
The Exception that Proves the Rule

The front page of the *London Review of Books* thirty years ago displayed a visual surprise, a full-page portrait of the mature Philip Roth, face forward with intense and glowering intelligence, displaying a forehead that had ascended to Alpine heights, and looking every inch the middle-aged man of letters.

There should, of course, be nothing surprising about a fifty-four-year-old man looking almost his age. But Philip Roth had been one of our great *young* writers for so long that his youth has become a permanent fixture in the consciousness of a generation of readers. For many of us, thinking of Roth as a youth was not innocent or unselfish. Unconsciously, we used the perception of Roth as a permanently young writer as a defense against the inevitability of middle age for all of us. Then, having invested in Roth's permanent youthfulness, the evidence of his progression into midlife forcefully reminds us of what we always should have known. And if adjustment to Portnoy's author as middle aged was difficult, what now that the bright young man of letters has turned eighty-one?

Having seemed for so long the exception to an ironclad rule of aging, Philip Roth became for many of us what I shall call the exception that proves the rule. He had been one of those people whose long run of youthfulness provides us with Peter Pan's irrational hope against our own aging. We are thus personally disappointed when the apparent exceptions inevitably fall prey to natural forces. Because we identify with these surrogates, we even experience something close to resentment when they become subject to temporal gravity. Aging, uncontrollable in our lives, is something we unconsciously regard as willful when it's committed by one of our ego ideals.

A short list of those who seemed so long to be modern American ever-young, those who have served as surrogates for our own Peter Pan ambitions is enormously miscellaneous. What else do Woody Allen, and the Beach Boys, surf rockers for half a century, have in common? Yet their youthfulness becomes an increasing part of their public importance with each passing year, as long as it remains.

The way in which we identify with these surrogate Peter Pans accounts for the inversion of normal emotional reactions we observe in ourselves and others. In circumstances of peer competition, if Joe Smith and Woody Allen are the same age but only Smith looks and feels his age, we expect Smith to be resentful of Allen's youthfulness and somewhat gratified when Allen visibly joins the club of the aging. But the process of identification inverts this. We take delight in Allen's youthfulness as evidence that being fifty, or sixty, or seventy need not involve crossing the more depressing frontiers of aging. We extract hope rather than competitive disappointment from the permanently youthful.

But the same process of identification leads to disappointment and bitterness when our designated exceptions cease to defy the laws of biology. Exempted from envy in their youth, the objects of our identification are resented for their eventual fallibility.

Just as each generation has its own small set of surrogate Peter Pans, so too do we seek out persons of great age and use them as temporary psychic exceptions to that most basic law of biological existence, mortality. The presidential telegrams and saccharine television news stories of Mrs. Fishbine's 107th birthday patronize us more than they patronize her. We celebrate great age for many reasons, but not the least of these is its function as a personal alternative to the shadow of imminent mortality. Persons of great age and great accomplishment, particularly those who continue to be zestful and productive, are surrogate immortals for us all. Pablo Casals, Pablo Picasso, Martha Graham, and Averell Harriman were recent examples. Harry Truman throughout the late 1950s and 1960s served a similar function for a number of then-older Americans. The comedians Jack Benny, Bob Hope, and George Burns self-consciously performed as surrogate immortals for decades. Apparent immortality became the central element of their public personas as time passed.

In the case of George Burns, his whole later career was shaped around the image of Methuselah as a mildly dirty old man. In his seventies, a comedian and performer whose public character previously had little of the bon vivant to it, suddenly added martinis and young girls to the soft-shoe song-and-dance routines and gentle humor of his prior forty years as a performer. He had become, in the literal sense, the personification of youthful old age rather than an extension of his earlier character structure.

The feelings of identification we express toward these surrogate immortals may explain what seem to be paradoxical patterns of public mourning. Many were utterly devastated when Jack Benny died in his eighties some years ago. The mourning may have been more pronounced for this wonderful symbol of continuity with the 1930s and 1940s because Jack Benny had become by the mid-1970s the exception that must prove the rule. If Jack Benny had died earlier the reaction might have been less. The longer the career and the happier the old age, the more many of us feel deprived with the inevitable passing.

Those who have been our principal evidence against death's necessity are most bitterly mourned in their passing. To have lived the best life, fought the hardest, and succeeded on all life's fronts is merely to flaunt the inevitability of death to that irrational element in us that must deny our mortality. With special force, the passage of the surrogate immortal produces self-mourning: "never send to know for whom the bell tolls; it tolls for thee."

19
The Arrogance of Nostalgia

I had last seen the woman I lunched with one December afternoon four-and-a-half years earlier on my first trip to Australia and in casual circumstances. At our first meeting, she had worn her hair flowing to her waist in pretty defiance of her junior executive station in government service. Sometime since then, on the way to more senior status, she had cut her hair to a sensible below-the-shoulder length.

My indefensible reaction, as a two-time visitor to her hemisphere, was to take this transition in style personally. The long hair had been so pretty, the effort so heroically against the centrifugal force of conventional upward mobility. How could she do this to me? To me, indeed. Here is the arrogance of nostalgia.

Nostalgia is, of course, everyone's secret emotional vice, the driving force that makes class reunions into psychodramas. It confers enormous importance on the people who were young with us or knew us then. Is there any other context in which our need to look good, to be successful, has such elemental emotional power?

The nostalgia of the high school reunion is both sweet and silly. Extreme cases may also be pathetic, if the hold exercised by the events and people of our particular past is too substantial. But arrogant?

What I call the arrogance of nostalgia is the conviction that the principal importance of other people in the world is the role that they have played in your life. This emotion is primitive, self-centered, and more pervasive than many of us would care to admit.

The arrogance of nostalgia is the organizing principle for class reunions. Mrs. Goldberg has taught high school Spanish for forty-five years, raised a family of her own, and now worries about the cost-of-living adjustment for her Social Security payments. But to the nostalgic, her true claim to significance on this earth centers on the part she played in an embarrassing episode of a long ago springtime. Gretchen Green's two marriages and long membership in the Church of Scientology are regarded as a mere aftermath to the central mission of her life, which was to be seventeen and pretty when the nostalgic was noticing.

Elements of this conceit extend beyond class reunions and are necessary to the self-regard of the healthy personality. But carried too far, this kind of nostalgia paralyzes the potential for further personal change. Assuming that the principal importance of other people on earth is the historic role they played in your life deprives other people of the capacity to have done anything important out of your presence. Feeling this way, we are incapable of appreciating who the people we cared about then really are now, because we cannot see the present texture of their lives, the people they have become.

The grandiose view of the nostalgics can also trap them into impossible feelings of responsibility for other people's lives. It can further lock them away from significant connections to the people and events of their own present. When this happens, the arrogance of nostalgia becomes the tyranny of nostalgia, it can rob nostalgics of appreciating that their present life is also a formative stage.

All of this sounds—and probably is—an overstatement for an emotional set that is usually regarded as innocuous. Nostalgia, even with its implicit arrogance, need not importantly distort the lives of others or confine the development of the nostalgic, as long as it does not overpower a sense of the priority of the present. The high school reunion threatens little if it remains an isolated emotional island in the sea of the contemporary.

At the root of nostalgia is healthy self-regard. To have respect for the particularity of the people we have become is to honor the events and personalities that played a part in our individual development. What makes the events of 1971 significant is the way in which they helped to shape us into the persons we, uniquely, have become. The girl next door was important, and you were important to her, as part of the mysterious process of becoming different from all the other people in the world. And we must honor those events to have a positive sense of individual specialness.

But the real danger of now pursuing the most beautiful girl in the world circa 1971, is not that she will have since run to fat, but that she will turn out to be ordinary in the cold light of adulthood. And the mix of emotions such an encounter can produce illustrates some of the crosscurrents of nostalgia.

The gracious, seemingly natural response to this kind of encounter, is to experience it as harmless. But the arrogance of nostalgia cuts in the other direction. Assuming that the two months that this she spent in your company in 1971 was the high point of this woman's life can have three negative consequences. First, with that kind of build-up there is the tendency to blame the other person for being anything short of wonderful.

Second, magnifying one's own importance in another's life also generates an outsized sense of obligation to match one's presumed significance. If May and June of 1971 were really the truly important parts of this woman's life, her only chance for happiness is your lifelong support. The tyranny of nostalgia is the obligation to live up to the inflated role one has imagined in the lives of figures who have played a role in one's personal history.

The third drawback of unconfined nostalgia is the limited capacity of the nostalgic to appreciate the circumstances of his or her current life as important. Magnifying the significance of distant personal history, and one's own importance in the lives of historic figures, crowds out current events.

Marcel Proust is an instructive case study. The only way to write seven volumes of *Remembrance of Things Past* is to take to your bed and spend the entire present time writing. Maybe it was worth the effort for this singular masterpiece, but the sacrifice of present concerns and connections rarely makes sense for the rest of us. The importance of persons and events is always and necessarily a matter of relative value. The more weight we place on the past, the less emphasis is available for the present.

All of this sounds ludicrous when baldly stated. The tyranny of nostalgia seems just a *reductio ad absurdum* from high school reunions to the petrification of personality. Yet the pulls in this direction are real, and they are better put in perspective if understood.

Honor of the significant past defeats its function when the contingencies of the long past repress our talent for continuing evolution. Each layer of the developing self deserves respect, but must leave emotional room for acknowledging the importance of succeeding stages. The denial of nostalgia negates the importance of the particular self; too much diminishes the continual process of the self's becoming.

How to strike the balance? The past can be appropriately honored by those who retain a sense of nostalgia for the present. Nineteen seventy-one can safely be the object of nostalgia for those who also consider 2015 to be an important formative period. A sense of history can be a positive force as long as it's balanced by a strong sense of the present as an important part of that history.

The Psychology of Commerce

20 • Be There or Be Square! The Existential Dilemma of Landmarks

21 • The Not-So-Secret Code of Real Estate Sales

22 • There May Always Be a Rolex

23 • Nonfiction Bestsellers for Next Year

24 • The Invisible Blessings of Prevention—And Why It's Dangerous to Ignore Them

20
Be There or Be Square!
The Existential Dilemma of Landmarks

Anyone who thinks that the only point of a grand tour of Europe is having a good time has never spent half a hot summer afternoon in line waiting to strain his neck muscles scanning the ceiling of the Sistine Chapel. The Americans who march grim-faced through this ritual have paid a pretty penny for the privilege. Why do most of them look so pained by the process? Why do they do it, when Waikiki is cheaper? Why not wait until next year when some Las Vegas casino will probably open its own tourist friendly version of the Sistine Chapel with central air conditioning and close-at-hand refreshments?

Even if the Disney Company were to open its own version of the Sistine Chapel or the Parthenon, I suspect that trooping off to see the original version would remain a compulsory rite of passage for those who can afford it, including hundreds of thousands of people who look for all the world as if they would rather be on the receiving end of root canal instead. If man is a pleasure-seeking creature, why does he seek out the anything-but-pleasant setting of mass tourism at high season? This is the conundrum of compulsive tourism.

Available evidence suggests that the force that impels so many of us to go on tours we hate is not mere cultural pretentiousness. It is not only the Louvre and the Sistine Chapel that command our attendance even if we don't much enjoy the process of visiting them. The Grand Canyon is a similar compulsory stop on American travels, not to mention the Eiffel Tower. Many of the least tasteful and educational sights on the planet have become landmarks in the great tradition of Mt.

Rushmore. The same impulse that pushes us toward the Sistine Chapel creates an audience for the two-headed cow at carnival sideshows.

Is it possible that those grim tourist faces are fakes, and everybody is having a wonderful time sweltering amidst the human pavement of the Vatican in mid-August? There are several reasons why this hypothesis is implausible. First, the discomfort on display in old world capitals is too powerfully authentic to be attributed to an acting job. Why fake pain when one is having a good time? The people in line at Disneyland do not often exude the aura of combat fatigue one sees in Florence, so there is no reason to suppose all the Florentine sad sacks are merely putting us on.

Of course there are some people who adore visiting landmarks. I married one. But when folks like her line up at the Sistine Chapel they are all aglow. Their behavior is not hard to explain and they are easy to tell from their more unfortunate fellow tourists. And for these enthusiastic lovers of celebrated tour stops, a return trip is a happy thought.

In contrast, the ultimate proof that a first visit to the Sistine Chapel is not a lark for the sad-sack tourist on a landmark march is the fact that very few of them seem eager to plan a return. But if the Sistine Chapel was worth $8,000 in effort this summer, why not pop in next year for a return engagement? For the same reason I would suggest that few of us pay twice to see the two-headed cow. We feel the need to see the landmark once, but there is no need to return for a second helping of a sight already seen. This is an important clue about why so many of us feel compelled to visit famous places on a like-it-or-not basis.

The felt need to see an important sight is a result of the existential dilemma of landmarks. Many people might have led more pleasant lives if the Eiffel Tower and the Great Pyramid of Cheops had never been built. But history did not cooperate with this preference, so the real choice that citizens confront is to either see the landmark or to miss it. If you go to the Great Pyramid, you may be inconvenienced and displeased. But if you do not go, you will miss seeing a place that the culture defines as important to visit. Thus, even if the cost and aggravation of getting to the pyramid is great, the disutility of never seeing it might be even greater.

Once some important landmark has become a part of our consciousness, it cannot be ignored—we must either see it or miss it. Each new icon pushes us further down a road we would just as soon not have to travel. In the pseudo-hip slogan of a recent period, the choice is to "be there or be square." Under those circumstances, the visitation of landmarks, like so much of modern life, is often the lesser of evils.

Now for the terrifying part. The supply of landmarks is not fixed, but is rather a social construct subject to expansion without notice. In this regard, each new landmark is a new difficulty for the cultural consumer, yet another place he or she either has to visit or has to miss. Indeed, there are economic and social incentives that have made the creation of landmarks into an industry in the modern world, the manufacture of things that must be seen. And each new landmark of this kind may be an inescapable obstacle in the individual's path to pleasure.

Under these circumstances, modern life can become a tug-of-war between the creators of landmarks and individuals trying to defend themselves from choosing yet again between a new outpost of compulsory visitation—or one more sight that if unseen will fuel a sense of personal inadequacy. The sad-faced tourists en route to the Sistine Chapel have discovered a new chapter heading in *Civilization and Its Discontents*. They are trying to live up to minimum standards of experience imposed by a culture with ever-expanding notions of all the things a good citizen must see at least once.

21
The Not-So-Secret Code of Real Estate Sales

All those English majors who didn't turn into Garrison Keillor the radio star may still have career opportunities that will fully employ their skills and talents—in real estate sales work.

Why should an English major sell real estate instead of life insurance or used cars? Because the peculiar nature of real estate advertising presents a communications problem that requires both skill with language and mastery of a whole set of specialized meanings that only apply in home selling. It is an English major's dream job.

The real estate sales agent must serve two often conflicting interests when telling the world about the properties he or she has on offer. The "listing" for the house is a necessary condition for making a commission—this assignment comes from the house owners who select the agent and can find another agent if they are dissatisfied. So the care and feeding of property owners must be an agent's high priority, and owners like to hear nice things said about their house. But somebody to purchase the house is also a prerequisite to the agent ever getting a sales commission and in order to maintain credibility with potential buyers, the agent must tell some version of the truth about the inventory. Saying nice things and telling the truth are often not equivalent tasks.

This leads to what can be called the descriptive dilemma of real estate sales. How is it possible to pay high compliments (to mollify owners) and communicate true facts (to signal buyers and maintain credibility) at the same time? The situation isn't hopeless because one part of the audience will have expert advisors to help them (prospective buyers have their own agents) while the other part of the audience (the sellers) must rely on the agent who is sending the message. So the double-duty code that develops is a set of precisely graded euphemisms that sound harmless or empty of meaning to home owners, yet brief buyers and their agents through code terms widely recognized by experts in the trade.

A beginner's introduction to these common code terms covers matters like size, obsolescence, and firmness of price. A brief review here will decode some hearty perennials.

Size matters in how a house is organized and in which rooms have space and an open appearance. But one can't write an ad that announces small living rooms or the seller will be offended. Yet euphemisms to warn about size are more widely understood in the trade than is the King's English. In any for sale home ad, "cozy" means "tiny," and "cute and cozy" means "very tiny." A "cozy" dining area means "seats two adults with low standards." A "cute and cozy" dining area promises claustrophobia for any adult. If you read these terms in house ads in Cape Town or Hamburg, you can probably rely upon the fact that the coded meanings are an international constant, they mean exactly the same as what they mean in Kansas City.

But what if the house hasn't been redecorated since the Eisenhower administration? "Traditional" homes in the Sunday paper are those with avocado and orange kitchen tiles and counters. For those houses where the major systems date back further, say to Herbert Hoover, the universal term in the Esperanto of real estate is "vintage home."

Home pricing is a delicate issue in the best of times and sending out signals to buyers is a necessary and risky business. How can an agent signal that there may be more than a little bargaining room in a current asking price? The absence of price flexibility is easy to announce (the word "firm" after the amount is often used) but an ad cannot announce the asking price is "not firm" so code euphemism is in demand. The most extreme signal for wiggle room in pricing is the phrase "motivated seller." Any buyer's agent responding to a "motivated seller" description by offering the asking price would be guilty of malpractice. For the seller's agent, the "motivated seller" description expresses faith in the magical powers of euphemism—no home owner would wish to be described as "desperate" or "asking way too much," but who could object to being called "motivated?" Here is the Triumph of Semantics over Substance.

The coded phrases that signal a property's state of disrepair are also important to maintain credibility with buyers and their agents. The table below provides some of the basic steps up the ladder of structural disability, with the left-hand column providing the code term and the right column providing its meaning.

Term	Translation
"Needs only Finishes"	Not as bad as it looks
"Needs TLC"	Just as bad as it looks
"Handyman Special"	Worse than it looks — real problems
"Contractor's Special"	Structural disaster

Of all the labels in the litany of real estate disrepair, the ubiquitous terms "fixer-upper" and "fixer" are the least communicative. They promise problems but don't provide guidance about any limits. Frustrated buyers will often conclude that there are only subtle differences between a "fixer upper" and a "burner downer."

Then there are the "good news/bad news" descriptions of housing amenities, where the adjectives in the description deflate the buyer's expectations. Thus, a "peek-a-boo" view of the ocean or lake is almost nonexistent, while a "filtered view" is slightly better for very tall people with exceptional eyesight.

A "splash pool" is a linguistic flourish to describe a uselessly puny backyard fixture. A splash pool might give your mother-in-law a soak but not leave room for any of her friends, and only the family cat can swim laps in it.

A "great starter home" will only suit the buyer who can't afford a "finisher home," but it is infinitely better than an "investor's special," a term that signals that nobody who can afford to buy it would ever want to live there.

This peculiar language of real estate sales is complex, stable over time, and well understood by its native speakers. The large number of double meanings not only keeps buyers and sellers content but also makes the buyer's real estate agent absolutely indispensable to anyone in the market to purchase real estate who only speaks ordinary English. Simple English is not now the language used for the advertising and selling of houses, and a vocabulary of plain meanings will probably never ever return.

22
There May Always Be a Rolex

The social history of machines that measure the passage of time is a fascinating subject, not least because it provides a fresh context for observing patterns in the general culture of modern society. The recent history of the wristwatch combines revolutionary technical and economic change with a set of social responses that tell us much about the psychology of materialism.

The technical revolution I have in mind is the production of a silicon-chip digital watch, an inexpensive, mass-produced wristwatch of phenomenal accuracy. The social responses to this development have been manifold, but one thing that has not happened is reduced social demand for expensive time machines that now have no significant technical advantage over cheap competition. The hyperexpensive premium watch has become a technical anachronism; nonetheless the luxury watch business keeps booming.

The coming of the digital timepiece was one of the first social transformations of the computer age. Just about when my children were ready to discern the code significance of the big hand and the little hand, things changed. The quartz time movement made phenomenally accurate time measure available to the mass market. The natural mode of conveying time information from these machines is, of course, a digital readout, a numerical statement of hour, minute, and second that is accurate to a standard no wristwatch of their grandfather's time could ever achieve. This digital phenomenon can be purchased by smart shoppers for less than ten dollars. Modest additional investment will produce a machine that measures month, day, and year, plays music, and will store frequently needed phone numbers. And of course, the era of the smartphone makes watches themselves unnecessary, although soon they too will be wearable on a wrist.

The quartz watch soon generated a universal culture of exact time among its users. When asked "what time is it?" my elder son at age ten would inspect his inexpensive digital and respond "7:47." No more round numbers as in "a quarter of eight" in the language or expectations of the first digital-watch generations. Time is something these kids expect can be precisely measured.

And measured on the cheap. By the early 1980s, there was no more social distinction in telling exact time. Where once the ability to keep highly accurate time on a wristwatch was the cachet of the expensive watch, exact time rapidly ceased performing the task of social differentiation because cheap digital watches flooded the market. Now that the poor man's watch or phone can tell perfect time, telling perfect time is no big deal.

One might think then that the digital era would mark the end of the $15,000 man's watch as status symbol, but not so. As the technical gap between Timex and Rolex narrowed, the social importance of the Rolex seems to have increased. Sales of four- and five-figure watches boomed throughout the generations after 1980, a period that also included reports of robbery killings to obtain Rolex watches. The counterfeit Rolex has become a staple item in the inventory of the street peddlers along with fool's gold chains and almost-diamonds. Why does this particular status symbol persist?

The current technical advantages of the super-premium watch are hardly an explanation of their desirability. When Hollywood agents take power lunches, it should not matter much that their $10,000 watches could withstand water pressure to a depth of 200 feet. Very few restaurants have ponds that deep. But people still hunger after the premium watch even as a pure status play.

This persistent appeal of the Rolex may tell an interesting tale of the relationship between technology and social meaning. Initially, what made the portable time machine an important arena for status comparisons was that really expensive watches told better time. That technical advantage generated the social value of the good watch. But once the social importance of the premium watch is established, the technical advantage need not be sustained for the social status significance to be maintained. The current generation of status conscious young people might believe that watches are important because they grew up in a culture where the watch was a status symbol. That alone may sustain the custom and the billion-dollar industry it spawned.

So our social totems may have a historical rationale but can also persist long after their original utility is lost in history, just as a spacecraft needs a powerful boost to break away from the earth's gravitational field but can then glide forever on its own. We may continue showing off with $10,000 diving watches well into this twenty-first century because ten-dollar machines did not tell good time in 1926.

There is one other way in which tradition and technology intersect instructively in the modern history of watches. Quartz technology can be harnessed in machines that display the time using the traditional hour, minute, and second hands rotating "clockwise" on a circular face. The readings one gets from these clock-style movements are actually less precise than digital readout but not much, and this old-fashioned face for the new-fashioned technology has become quite popular. In particular, most of the super expensive quartz watches use the clock display so that current premium watches tell time a tad less precisely than their cheaper digital cousins. But technical advantage may be more easily sacrificed to aesthetic considerations now that the accuracy of watches has ceased to distinguish expensive machines from cheap ones.

Students of social trend should take note of this aspect of the recent history of watches because the pattern may be a general one. As technical prowess is more easily achieved, it may become less important to its users. There may be more room for nontechnical distinction, more importance for non-technical fashion in a society that has come to take its technology for granted.

23
Nonfiction Bestsellers for Next Year

Fueled by my own frequent appearance on least-seller lists, I have long been fascinated by how other folks make millions by selling nonfiction books to mass markets. Much of the time, the formula is simple: find a topic of personal interest to millions of people and write a book that promises them hope of personal improvement or at least edification. But the field is getting crowded. Reading titles on bestseller lists over the last decade, one would suppose the American public is approaching physical and spiritual perfection, sorting out relationships while running twelve miles a day.

This presents something of a commercial problem. Writing the seventeenth book on creative aggression is by no means the guarantee of riches that greeted earlier entrants to the tough love field. With so many self-help and education areas getting saturated, the new strategy is finding the right topic for a mass audience that others have missed. Having given the matter much thought, I submit the following entrants for next year's best-seller list:

When Good Things Happen to Bad People. If God is in His heaven, how are we ordinary schmoes to deal with why the absolute bastard down the street wins the state lottery? Why do cocaine dealers get to buy condos in Maui? The project requires a minister, priest, or rabbi brave enough to tackle this perennial and perplexing problem. The potential market is enormous, because anyone who thinks of himself as virtuous encounters this problem twice a month. Most of us have it in the family.

Eat Right to Keep Fat. Nutritional guides have always been marketing dynamite, but this field has crowded with particular alacrity. Food guides to losing weight, running well, building muscle, avoiding cancer, and remaining forever young can hardly be considered novelty items. But the voluntarily obese, fat people who don't mind being fat, have been ignored, and one doesn't have to hire a market research organization to realize the nutritional needs of a significant segment of the American population is being ignored. Think of it: low cholesterol binge foods; a balanced diet on 4,000 calories a day; smorgasbord without heartburn.

A Social Manual for Creative Celibacy. Voluntary celibacy has proceeded from monastic ritual to social fashion. But rejecting sex still requires finding like-minded people to share one's life. These folks need strategies: how to meet, how to make sure a respective partner is of the same persuasion, social graces without sex, dealing with lapses and infidelity. The ideal author for this would be a celibate psychiatrist, if one can be found.

Doctor Zuckerman's Guide to Medical Impotence. The plethora of medical advice books currently break into three categories. One is a conventional medical account of what can be done to cure various ailments. A second type of book is written by a doctor who believes he or she alone possesses the correct cure to one or a number of diseases. The third usual book is a tantrum about how doctors screw up in the sense of making avoidable mistakes while treating patients. What's missing is a book about the conditions for which even the best medicine can't do a damn thing. From uncomplicated arthritis through the common cold, the American public is waiting to hear about when not to see even Dr. Kildare. For $19.95.

The Loser's Guide to Personal Happiness. The books that guarantee making millions in real estate, getting love letters from famous actresses, or winning the Pulitzer Prize for Fiction are a pyramid swindle. Everyone can't win. And if everyone were to become hyperconfident and assertive, the homicide rate would increase dramatically. This dynamite new book will take on an opposite tack. It will help losers find true serenity in the conditions of their lives? The joys of being demoted; low income as tax shelter; being dumped as a growth experience. The examples multiply.

There is however, a paradox confronted in finding an author to write a successful book about the joys of losing. Wouldn't he be, by definition, a winner? Well, what about a guy, now on the least-seller list, who announces in the Introduction that he sold all the rights to the book for a song before it came out? Interested publishers could contact my agent, if I had one.

24
The Invisible Blessings of Prevention— And Why It's Dangerous to Ignore Them

In 1955, 166 million citizens were exposed to the streets and highways of the United States and 36,688 of them were killed in traffic, a tragic but seemingly unavoidable byproduct of an essentially automotive civilization. The culture was torn between thinking of road deaths as "accidents" beyond human will and centering the blame on bad drivers. It was said back then that "the most dangerous part in the automobile is the nut behind the wheel."

Fast-forward to 2010. There were almost twice as many participants on the great American auto strada, and they drove almost six times more miles as they did in 1955—but the body count had gone down by almost 5,000. We still lose many too many lives in traffic, but the arithmetic of improvements in traffic fatalities is nothing short of astonishing. If the death rate per million miles driven had remained at its 1955 level, 191,000 of us would die each year. So the 82 percent reduction in the death rate from driving (from 6.06 per 100,000,000 miles driven to 1.11) by 2010 saved more than 153,000 American lives every year.

What accounts for this huge drop in the death rate per million miles driven? A great variety of changes share the credit including more divided highways, a reduction in alcohol-related fatalities, better emergency medicine, and vast improvements in the design of automobiles and of the roads they use. Ours is now a republic of seat belts, air bags, padded steering wheels, interstate highways, tough and high-priority drunk driving enforcement and traffic safety legislation. But behind all of this was the game-changing creation of government efforts to make cars, drivers, and roads less dangerous. It is probable that the cumulative impact of all these changes saved a million lives in the twelve years after 2000.

A government program that saved a million lives in just twelve years? Why was this one of the best-kept secrets of modern life? Part of the low visibility of improved auto safety is the tendency we all have to soon forget the problems we had before conditions improved. The deaths and injuries that remain concern us much more than the statistical improvements over earlier times. Mothers Against Drunk Driving doesn't place their emphasis on the good news.

But there is also a paradox of prevention that leads us to undervalue strategies that prevent harms from happening. When science improves our ability to treat and cure diseases, the beneficiaries of such progress are easy to identify. If penicillin cures your child's pneumonia, we know who was helped and how. When blood sugar monitors and bioengineered insulin improve the lives of diabetics, they leave clear indications of their efficacy. But the 10,000 or so drivers who don't get killed on two-lane highways because divided highways were built for them don't know who they are. And the suspicious parents who resent compulsory polio and diphtheria inoculations do not see any clear connection between a painful shot and any apparent benefit to their child. Even if their Jennifer would have been the unlucky child to contract diphtheria, this is not something that parents who resent governmental coercion can ever learn (before it's too late).

And while diabetics who now use improved monitors and medicines know they are benefitting, any children who might someday benefit from a limit on supersized sugary drinks will probably never know that their weight and health were affected. Prevention policy is a secret agent that often leaves no calling card. Its good works are likely to be ignored by everybody but the statisticians and experts who are paid to keep track of aggregate costs and benefits.

Two other spectacular examples of the invisible blessings of prevention concern death rates from heart disease and fatalities from commercial air travel. In the United States at mid-century, fatal heart attacks among men on the threshold of middle age were not uncommon and the numbers after age 45 were even higher. The annual heart death rate in 1955 for males ages 35–44 was 113 per 100,000, so that one percent of these men would die of heart disease in that decade. The yearly rate for men aged 45–54 was 441 per 100,000, so that more than one in every 25 men became a heart-related death in the ten years prior to turning 55.

Fast-forward to 2010: both of the 1955 fatality rates had dropped by more than 80 percent. The death rate for men aged 25-44 dropped from over 110 each year to under 20, an 83 percent decline for a terrible outcome that we used to consider the product of problematic genes and bad luck but hardly the stuff of public policy. The much higher death rates among men aged 45-54 fell just as fast; the 2010 death rate was less than a fifth of its 1955 total (78 per 100,000 versus 441).

Decades of hectoring about cigarettes and blood pressure and salt intake and blood fats had played a major role in reducing premature deaths from the nation's number one killer. But most of those who would have dropped dead in 1955 but now live normally in the twenty-first century don't realize that their lives have been saved. So here is another nearly invisible blessing that came from concerned public and social campaigns.

A final example of easy-to-overlook progress concerns commercial air travel. Frightening as it may seem to jump through the clouds at hundreds of miles per hour, commercial flights have been pretty safe for a long time. During the five years at the beginning of the jet era (1960–1964), there was one fatal crash for every 178,000 commercial flights—so even the frequent fliers of 50 years ago had much more reason to worry about heart disease and auto crashes then commercial airline crashes.

But massive investments in regulation, product improvement, air traffic control, and aircraft safety systems have been made and those investments have paid conspicuous dividends. The five years from 2006 to 2010 produced an average U.S. rate of fatal accidents only one-twentieth of that in the early 1960s—0.28 per million flights instead of 5.6. We solved 95 percent of a very scary problem.

Because public support for effective programs of prevention depends on trust in experts or government, the cynical second decade of the twenty-first century may be a dangerous time for the public health and safety. The million Americans who are alive today because of the cumulative improvements in roads and cars and driving don't know who they are and thus they might be skeptical of the very policies that saved their lives. Unless we learn to trust statistics and experts and government, it will be necessary to massively educate the general public. Since the achievements of prevention programs are not visible to the man on the street, policies that could keep millions of us safe and healthy may consistently fail to gain support in democratic politics.

*　*　*

About the Author

Frank Zimring has spent most of his professional life as a Professor of Law at the University of Chicago and the University of California, Berkeley. His major scholarly interests are criminal justice, juvenile justice, and efforts to control violent crime. Much of his published work concerns juvenile courts and adolescent development, the death penalty, crime prevention, and imprisonment. Since the early 1980s, however, he has also written a series of essays on what he calls "his second career, and everybody else's second career, the meanings and lessons that come from the hard work of becoming an adult in the modern world." Those essays are the memos from midlife collected in this volume. Examples of Zimring's writings are reproduced in nine college writing texts.

Professor Zimring is married to Michal Crawford Zimring and has two adult children.

Visit us at *www.quidprobooks.com*.

www.ingramcontent.com/pod-product-compliance
Lightning Source LLC
Chambersburg PA
CBHW071215160426
43196CB00012B/2318